GESTA HUMANORUM

GESTA HUMANORUM
STUDIES IN THE HISTORICIST MODE

ROY HARVEY PEARCE

UNIVERSITY OF MISSOURI PRESS
COLUMBIA, 1987

Library of Congress Cataloging-in-Publication Data
Pearce, Roy Harvey.
    Gesta humanorum: Studies in the historicist mode.
    Includes index.
    1. American literature—History and criticism.
I. Title.
PS121.P38   1987810'.9   87-5091
ISBN 0-8262-0637-9 (alk. paper)

∞™ This paper meets the minimum requirements of
the American National Standard for Permanence of
Paper for Printed Library Materials, Z39.48, 1984.

For permissions statements, see the author's Foreword,
pp. xiii-xvi.

For Stephen Gilman (1917-1986)
La Tierra es gran aventura.

FOREWORD

1

The studies collected here are informed by a conviction (deriving from a fact) that works of literature, like all human acts, however recorded, are inextricably implicated in the historical situations out of which they come. (Indeed, the recording itself is integrally a mode of implication.) Full comprehension of those situations—especially in critically determining instances—is thus a necessary condition of that understanding which makes interpretation possible. Such interpretation, so achieved, I take in turn to be a necessary condition of sociocultural responsibility—of belief, commitment, and action: what I continue to term Humanism. In History, not Dreams, begins—only begins—such responsibility. Thus my title and subtitle.

There is nowadays an increasing range of Historicisms—"New Historicisms," to adapt the title of a book published in 1972 and also of a series about to be initiated by the University of California Press.[1] These Historicisms may be sorted out, I think, according to the sort of anthropology (or anthropological commitments) in which they are grounded. Some, concerned with the problem of "representations," are grounded in forms of Symbolic Anthropology, so-called, in which language (or code) figures preemptively in delimiting and also in enabling all modes of discourse.[2] (Wallace Stevens has a poem called "Men Made Out of Words" on which some interpreters of this persuasion might

1. See Wesley Morris, *Toward a New Historicism* (Princeton: Princeton University Press, 1972). But of course we should grant that Morris has had some characteristically post-structuralist second thoughts: *Friday's Footprint* (Columbus: Ohio State University Press, 1979). The forthcoming (as of January 1987) University of California Press series is thus introduced by its editor, Stephen Greenblatt:

> Literary criticism is witnessing, in strikingly original ways, a return to the historical embeddedness of literary productions, while the study of history is witnessing innovative explorations of the symbolic construction of reality. This series highlights the emergence of a powerful new interpretive paradigm with works directed not only to literature but to politics, social practices, religious beliefs, and cultural conflicts.

2. See the journal *Representations*, edited by Svetlana Alpers and Stephen Greenblatt, for some brilliant examples of this mode. From the anthropological perspective, see James Clifford and George E. Marcus, eds., *Writing Culture: The Poetics and Politics of Ethnography* (Berkeley: University of California Press, 1986).

vii

well meditate.) Another form is grounded in Althusserian neo-Marx-
ism and presumes, via "mediations" (a form of what used to be called
"conventions"), a "political unconscious"—in effect, a collective
unconscious from the power and form of which ultimately derive all
human "productions."[3] Some, embracing as do I the recent happy
legitimation of the concept of Ideology, are grounded in an
Anthropology that is, in my opinion, too often smothered by a com-
bination of Geertzian and Frankfort School anthropology and of
Annales Historiography.[4] Some would, using Foucault's work as

3. The most powerful work here—in its power empowering profound disagree-
ment—is Fredric Jameson, *The Political Unconscious* (Ithaca: Cornell University Press,
1981).

4. See, for example, Myra Jehlen, "Introduction: Beyond Transcendence," in Sac-
van Bercovitch and Myra Jehlen, eds., *Ideology and Classic American Literature* (New
York: Cambridge University Press, 1986), pp. 1-18. See also the powerful commentary
of Louis Montrose, who senses himself, quite rightly, as one kind of a new historicist,
in "Renaissance Literary Studies and the Subject of History," *English Literary Renaissance* 16 (1986):5-12:

> By representing the world in discourse, texts are engaged in constructing the world
> and in accommodating their writers, performers, readers, and audiences to positions
> within it. In recent years, the vexed but indispensable term "ideology" has, in it most
> general sense, come to be associated with the processes by which social subjects are
> formed, re-formed, and enabled to perform as conscious agents in an apparently mean-
> ingful world.

In the same issue of *English Literary Renaissance*, Jean E. Howard, extrapolating
from the work of Montrose and also from that of Don E. Wayne and Stephen Greenblatt, puts the matter quite straightforwardly and so lets us detect its problematics:

> I take, then, that as starting points a new historical literary criticism assumes two
> things: (1) the notion that man is a construct, not an essence; (2) that the historical
> investigator is likewise a product of his history and never able to recognize otherness in
> its pure form, but always in part through the framework of the present. This last point
> leads one to what is perhaps the crux of any "new" historical criticism, and that is to the
> issue of what one conceives history to be: a realm of retrievable fact or a construct made
> up of textualized traces assembled in various configurations by the historian/inter-
> preter. (23-24)

Later, on the basis of her assumptions "that the ideological is everywhere and
traverses literature as surely as other modes of representation," she asks the primary
question: "does literature have a special way of treating the ideological?" (28).

One notes in Montrose "texts," not "authors," and wants an even implicit definition of "conscious." The "ideological" criticism called for by this mode of "historicism" affords no account of "intentionality," even of the "text" itself, since "social
subjects" are "formed" but apparently do not themselves "form." And in Howard
there is apparently no interest in the possible "psychological" components of her
"constructs," as there is none in Montrose's "constructing," presumably because the

model, boldly pragmatize it, reconstrue the work of Kenneth Burke, and so invent a History that, though discontinuous in its nature, has its origins solely in the present—presumably (and obviously) because we can act only in the present.[5]

These are, of course, overlapping categories—our profession happily being one of overlaps. For who can define precisely Humanities, Humanistic Studies, *Sciences Humaines*, and *Geisteswissesenschaften*? Who can define precisely Interpretation? What all the "New Historicisms" do emphasize, however variously, is the embeddedness of literature and all discourse in their sociocultural situations, defined historically.

It is not my concern here to develop an analysis of the various and varying "New Historicisms" I characterize above, although I do think that their practitioners might well take more heed of their own history—that is, of their own historicity. I here observe only that these practitioners too often have an awkward and embarrassing difficulty with the concept of Self—and, along with it, with the concept of specifically human intentionality. Caught in this predicament, I think, they often surrender in advance to one or another of the various Post-Structuralisms that they (fatefully) want both to oppose and to absorb. I, however, unabashedly admit to holding to a belief in Presence, Logocentrism, and, as I have said, Humanism. I shall presently say Humanisms.

So much for hortatory polemics, although they are to a degree continued in the second piece in this collection. My obligation here is to set forth conspectively and briefly *my* sense of Historicism and the historicist mode, hence of the sort of anthropology in which they are grounded and the method which that grounding enables and demands.

---

admission of such components would court the danger of some sort of "essentialism." In Montrose and Howard, of course, there is more than one Historicism involved. Thus the matter of the overlapping of the various historicist modes that I note below. As the length of this note indicates, I find the "ideologized" historicist mode nearest to my own, richest for me in my attempt to define my own, although my own does in fact assume a certain "essentialism" as regards human nature.

5. See Frank Lentricchia, *After the New Criticism* (Chicago: University of Chicago Press, 1980); *Criticism and Social Change* (Chicago: University of Chicago Press, 1983); and "The Return of William James," *Cultural Critique* 4 (1986):5-31.

The *method* of my version of the mode is expounded in the first study in this collection.

My studies have as their matrix psychological anthropology—what in the past was called culture-personality theory, what in the past I tended to understand as an analogue of existentialism and not vice-versa. Accordingly, they proceed from the assumption that there are inevitable tensions, never (because of our biological limitations) to be altogether resolved, between self and culture—between, that is to say, the demands on the ego set by the id and those set by the superego. (This, because it leads to consciousness of self and self-consciousness, is the sum of what, traditionalist that I am, I have called Humanitas.) It is specifically in works of literature, I believe (and also on the analyst's couch?), that those tensions are most profoundly explored, enacted, and set forth, since works of literature have as their empowering agent the writer's opportunity—or gift—to maximize the capacity to employ fictions in the use of language. (The freedom gained by fictiveness might well have as its analogue—by no means equivalent to or identical with—the freedom granted by the psychoanalytic transaction.)

All documents, however recorded, of course employ fictions—the degree to which this is so being one of the primary concerns of those who now think about "discourse analysis." But in my opinion there is a range of uses—from the (almost) totally self-controlled, thus self-reflexive, use in pure mathematics to that use which is (almost) totally out of control, the language of schizophrenia. Somewhere along this range there is the use of language in literature. And surely that use is nearer to the use in schizophrenia (mediated by the use of language in nonsense?) than it is to the use in pure mathematics. Thus the focus in the aesthetics derived from ego psychology—itself complementary to psychological anthropology—on controlled regression and the like: the capacity of the artist (in this collection read: writer) to make contact with the preconscious, fantasy, the "asocial," the purely individuated—only, in a formalized, highly structured and controlled mode, to report back to us, his (read: his or her) readers, the resulting tension between self and culture and its meaning and import for us. In so doing, he (read: he or she) signals to his exegete and critic that culture (the superego system) is at once enabling and disabling, even as personality (the id/ego system) is at once enabling and disabling. Thus the writer is inevitably, via his control within the freedom of fictiveness, both the advocate and the adversary of his culture. The "formal" means the writer uses in his mode of discourse are all means toward his necessary fictions—such devices (prosodic schemes, inversions and controversions of syntax, tropes, plots, and so forth) being means toward a necessary fictionality. Out of all this comes what Hawthorne termed "the truth of the human heart" and James, after him, "the deeper psychology." I am not embarrassed to use these terms.

All literary discourse, I believe, even that which overtly declares otherwise, is anti-utopian—in the sense that it derives from that aspect of the human condition which instructs us that we must aspire to utopias but that, locked in our historically definable conflicted awareness of the tension between self and culture, we must resign ourselves to being failed utopians—often, in that resignation, with a certain feeling of triumph or joy, because we have tried so hard and because we have *understood* our failure. I cannot do better here than to quote that great failed utopian, Herbert Marcuse, in his final testimony, *The Aesthetic Dimension: Toward a Critique of Marxist Aesthetics*:

> But even such a society [that is, one organized according to a new socialist reality principle] would not signal the end of art, the overcoming of tragedy, the reconciliation of the Dionysian and the Apollonian. Art cannot sever itself from its origins. It bears witness to the inherent limits of freedom and fulfillment, to human embeddedness in nature. In all its ideality art bears witness to the truth of dialectical materialism—the permanent non-identity between subject and object, individual and individual.[6]

I venture to say that "dialectical materialism" is a cover term here for a phenomenon—our situation in history and its tension between self and culture—that goes beyond Marxism as such. Nonetheless, Marcuse makes it clear that subject and object—individual as "free" self and individual as "acculturated" self—embedded in their historical condition, needfully striving toward a never-to-be-achieved integration and reconciliation, are the stuff of all human discourse. But it is in literary discourse, freed by its fictive reality principle (which Marcuse came only late to grant), that we can most fully comprehend the subject-object relationship and so (perhaps) comprehend ourselves in the act of being

6. (Boston: Beacon Press, 1978), p. 29

ourselves—or, because the comprehension is mediated by art, our possible, because fictive, selves. In effect, we introject a sense of the radically
different yet authentic other. In this comprehension—fictively structured as it is—lie the satisfactions that derive from art. And this comprehension is a form of what is called Humanism.

2

But there are two Humanisms, I believe, what I have come to term
the Humanism of the One and the Humanism of the Many—that is,
Humanism overdetermined by Self and Humanism overdetermined by
Culture. The studies collected here are mainly concerned with that pre-
dominating Humanism, for well and for ill, in American society in its
history, the Humanism of the One. They are thus intended to be critical
inquiries, assessments of achievements, often at the expense of failures.
There is, I have discovered in trying to comprehend my world—the
world of my history—in its literary and subliterary expressions, an abiding sense of the Humanism of the One insufficiently complemented and
complicated by a sense of the Humanism of the Many, a sense of Self
insufficiently complemented and complicated by a sense of Culture.

Hawthorne, in my reading, can in his mode of fiction, the Romance,
only *desiderate* that new form of marriage which will signal a maturing
of American culture—this in *The House of the Seven Gables*. In *The
Blithedale Romance*, via a voyeuristic poetaster, he would have us discover
ourselves as childlike utopians who cannot conceive of failure, much less
confront it. Whitman cannot find the means to hold on to his exclusive
commitment to the Humanism of the One, celebrated in the 1855 and
1860 *Leaves of Grass*, and so gradually yields himself altogether, and
helplessly, to the Humanism of the Many. Mark Twain, as he
increasingly agonizes over American society, creates a Huck Finn who is
fooled, largely by himself, into thinking that his kind of Humanism (of
the One) can survive entirely free of the burden of the Humanism of the
Many; Mark Twain in high irony lets us know better, once we understand the historistic dimensions of *Adventures of Huckleberry Finn*,
especially those of the Evasion chapters. Wallace Stevens steadily and
heroically projects the idea of the Humanism of the One toward a virtually suicidal end, thus exposing at once its mightiest capabilities and
its fatal weaknesses. Earlier than all of these, Revolutionary War poets,

overwhelmingly involved in their version of the Humanism of the Many, write poems that, because they are in fact totally overwhelmed, are quite vapid, tensionless. And last in this collection there are the New Poets, those of our quite recent past, most of them still writing, who strive for a mode (I have called it dialogic) that would project them toward a union, necessarily marked by struggle and tension, of the Humanism of the One and the Humanism of the Many. Thus this collection depicts Progress—of a sort.

Writing this Foreword, I discover that I here have mainly pointed out cultural failures. Writing the studies themselves, I tried to point out successes, those successes that, since they complement cultural failures, are the successes of art, itself of course a mode of culture. In the process, I tried to find those quite specific critically determinative sociocultural, historical situations out of which the writings I have studied have come, so to see how those situations (which I would declare are in effect ideological) have in good part made the achievements of those writings both possible and impossible. The Humanism of the One, that is to say, has empowered that kind of literature which, in its successes, is, for well and for ill, "American." In its history, so these studies argue, American literature begins (only begins—the rest being art) to discover the dimensions of cultural possibility and impossibility. Out of that discovery comes the responsibility it has put upon us.

Writing to his Bowdoin College classmate Longfellow on 22 November 1855, thanking him for a copy of *Hiawatha*, Hawthorne declared, "I love America but do not like it. Pray don't tell anybody this." Well, writing the studies that follow, I have tried to tell this, via a series of Interpretations, to anybody who would read me.

3

Seven of these studies have been published before, pretty much in the form in which they are here reprinted. I thank the editors and publishers responsible for allowing me to reprint:

"Gesta Humanorum: Notes on the Humanist as Witness," *Daedalus* 99 (1970):435-50.
"Poetry, and Progress/Criticism and Culmination," in E. C. Blessington and G. Rotella, eds., *The Motive for Metaphor: Essays on*

Modern Poetry (Boston: Northeastern University Press, 1983), pp. 112-23.

"Poetry, Revolution, and the Age of Paine," *San Jose Studies* 2 (1976):6-25.

"Day-Dream and Fact: The Import of *The Blithedale Romance*," in K. H. Baldwin and D. K. Kirby, eds., *Individual and Community: Variations on a Theme in American Fiction* (Durham, N.C.: Duke University Press, 1975), pp. 49-63.

"Whitman Justified: The Poet in 1855," *Critical Inquiry* 8 (1981):83-97.

"Yours Truly, Huck Finn," in R. Sattelmeyer and J. D. Crowley, eds., *One Hundred Years of Huckleberry Finn* (Columbia: University of Missouri Press, 1985), pp. 313-24.

"Toward the New Poetry: The Burden of Romanticism," *Iowa Review* 2 (1971):199-218.

"The Cry and the Occasion: Rereading Stevens"—much of which has been previously unpublished—borrows from "'Anecdote of the Jar': An Iconological Note," *Wallace Stevens Journal* 1 (1977):64-65; "The Cry and the Occasion: 'Chocorua to Its Neighbor,'" *Southern Review* 15 (1979):776-91; and "'The Emperor of Ice Cream': A Note on the Occasion," *Wallace Stevens Journal* 3 (1979):53-55.

"A Sense of the Present: Hawthorne and *The House of Seven Gables*," previously unpublished, had its origins in a Longest Lecture given at the University of Mississippi 17 November 1975. I continue to be grateful for the occasion.

(Oil on Canvas, 10 $^1/_8$ x 19 $^5/_8$, 1855: Gift of Matthew Vassar) is by courtesy of Vassar College Art Gallery, Poughkeepsie, New York.

R.H.P.
January 1987

CONTENTS

I.

GESTA HUMANORUM:

TOWARD METHOD

"He seeks
For a human that can be accounted for."
—Stevens, "Looking across the Fields
and Watching the Birds Fly"

1

GESTA HUMANORUM:
THE HUMANIST AS WITNESS

1

I mean to suggest by my main title the utopian aspirations of the humanistic studies, concerned with those human deeds so important in their history that they compel us to know them for what they were and continue to be. We would learn to assent to them—at most, as possibly our own deeds, and at least, as deeds done on our behalf. In the process (it is important to emphasize that humanistic study is a process, an act, itself a deed amenable to further humanistic study), we hope to discover and confirm alternate modes of what we take to be authentically human. My subtitle qualifies this utopianism with the individual humanist's acknowledgment of his limitations: His is after all but one perspective, that of the scholar whose special expertise demands that he bear witness to what he has learned.

Whatever the limited perspective of the individual humanist, today he is willing, even eager, to conceive of the scope of humanistic studies as extending beyond the humanities as traditionally set, at least into the social sciences. Indeed, he discovers that the modern anthropologist's definition of culture may well be his own:

> Our ideas, our values, our acts, even our emotions, are, like our nervous system itself, cultural products—products manufactured, indeed, out of tendencies, capacities, and dispositions with which we were born, but manufactured none the less. Chartres is made of stone and glass. But it is not just stone and glass; it is a cathedral, and not only a cathedral, but a particular cathedral built at a particular time by certain members of a particular society. To understand what it means, to perceive it for what it is, you need to know rather more than the generic

properties of stone and glass and rather more than what is common to all cathedrals. You need to understand also—and . . . most critically— the specific concepts of the relations between God, man, and architecture that, having governed its creation, it consequently embodies. It is no different with men: they, too, every last one of them, are cultural artifacts.[1]

Such a definition of culture at the beginning entails such a definition of man at the end, or vice versa. More important, it is based on a conception of a continuing transaction between man and those "objects" of the world, including other men, that constitute his culture. This transaction might well be described as a continuing "subjectivization" of the "objective." The objects of culture were created by human deeds, *gesta humanorum*; their function in man's life can be known precisely only if the humanist, like the anthropologist, studies them as *continuing* deeds. He recovers a sense of their life in the past so as to render a continuing possibility of and for life in the present.

The humanist then has as his concern an overwhelming panoply of activities—the work of artists and artisans, poets and politicians, scientists and sociologists, reporters and reverends—as evidence of their deeds comes to him in documents. His task is to discover which are the most important documents and then to learn to understand and interpret them. He may well confine himself to just one class of documents—paintings, houses, poems, campaign speeches, experiments in molecular biology, editorials, or sermons; or he may collocate such documents and try to see how they are related to one another, how together they are expressive of the achievement of the human spirit. His is an attempt to discover the world as human, so the more fully to humanize himself and his readers, auditors, or viewers.

Here the humanist discovers that his fundamental charge is to bear witness. As an "expert witness," in the legal sense, and not a direct witness of the original deed, he must study the document(s) which that deed brought forth and testify as to origin, meaning, and significance. Beyond the "legal" implication of his calling as witness, there is a "religious" implication, religious if only in the sense that the humanist has a commitment to the idea of man and the life of the human spirit— *humanitas* as an absolute value. He may not like what his studies tell

1. Clifford Geertz, "The Impact of the Concept of Culture," in J. R. Platt, ed., *New Views of the Nature of Man* (Chicago: University of Chicago Press, 1965), p. 114.

him; he may indeed discover that the document and the deed it projects somehow violate the very idea of man to which he is committed, narrowing rather than extending the possibility of full and authentic selfhood in society. Nonetheless, the scholarship of the humanist is grounded in that rigorous set of disciplines by which he was taught to discover and tell the truth.

An idea central to humanistic studies since the Renaissance compels the humanist to bear witness to *gesta humanorum*, that is, the dignity of man. We may no longer find supportable the claims of Pico's fifteenth-century oration on the subject: "O supreme generosity of God the Father, O highest and most marvelous felicity of man! To him it is granted to have whatever he chooses, to be whatever he wills." We can no longer afford Pico's God-centered aristocratic individualism. Products and producers of culture, we take a somewhat more cautionary and, at the same time, more expansive view and accordingly find that the scope of our interests and concerns has likewise become at once more cautionary and more expansive:

> Men need, as much as they need clothes, a sense of dignity and of purpose; and therefore they need systems which protect and legitimize such a sense, and a language and clusters of concepts which enable them to share that sense with others and to receive from others the reassurance of awareness that the sense is shared and that one is not, as one had feared, naked and alone. . . . There is something affected, and pretentious, in claiming to despise the expression, in great numbers of human beings, of general human needs which the scoffer necessarily shares. . . . One cannot refute the expression of a need, and although one can remove the need itself, there are some needs which can only be removed by death. One such need seems to be the need for dignity.[2]

The humanist's sense of the dignity of man is nonetheless firm for being somewhat muted. Above all, it demands of him that he deepen and enlarge his conception of *gesta humanorum* and thus of the documents which it is his special charge as humanist to discover, preserve, and elucidate. His task now as ever is to design and carry out those principles of elucidation deriving from his deepened and enlarged role as witness.

2. Conor Cruise O'Brien, "Imagination and Politics," in J. C. Laidlaw, ed., *The Future of the Modern Humanities* (Cambridge: Modern Humanities Research Association, 1969), pp. 77-78.

2

I assume that it is unarguable that the first stage in any humanistic study is that of exegesis—teaching oneself to understand the documents with which one is concerned. This, of course, is "scholarship"—the establishment of a correct text, the mastery of its vocabulary, grammar, and syntax, the identification of the system of conventions of the culture for and in which it was made, and so on. To know how to find and use such data is a necessary condition (as it were, the underside of the iceberg) of understanding and interpretation. "Understanding" I differentiate from "interpretation" because understanding involves the focusing on one document at a time—the attempt to know the document in and of itself. Interpretation—which is my main concern here—consists in moving beyond (but necessarily *via*) understanding to the interrelating of documents (of the same class, of different classes, or of both) in such a way as to know them in their historically definable sociocultural matrix. Here we come to what I shall call the problem of implication.

My perspective is that of a literary humanist, whose concern is to study literary documents such as poems. Poems, modern criticism tells us, are documents so made that we must perforce understand them intrinsically, in and of and for themselves. Indeed, recent linguistic theory has defined poetry as language so used as to call attention to itself.[3] In poetry certain aspects of language (for example, simile and metaphor, metrical effects inherent in the language, and grammaticality itself) are used to exploit the capacity to make fictions: statements not, strictly speaking, subject to the correspondence theory of truth. There is a kind of centripetal movement, whereby linguistic meanings and usages in ordinary discourse are focused, intermeshed, and made into a new self-sustaining whole; and it is toward the elucidating and grasping of this whole that literary critical understanding is directed. The language of a poem exists independently of the poetic context in which it is used; prior to a literary understanding of the poem, the humanist must master that language in its extra-poetic context: This is "scholarship." The new whole is a special kind of human deed in the knowledge of which—in and of and for itself—we can rest satisfied, if only for a

3. For a brilliantly succinct exposition of this view, see Roman Jakobson, "Concluding Statement: Linguistics and Poetics," in T. A. Sebeok, ed., *Style in Language* (Cambridge: MIT Press, 1960), pp. 350-77.

while. Once we know what the poem is ("means" in this order of discourse comes to equal "is"), we want to know what it *does*. At that point we perforce begin to interpret. We may ask questions of the poem, questions deriving from our situation in history and not from the poem in its own: How does the poem relate to other poems and to other kinds of documents? What light does the poem throw on our systems of belief and commitment, taken either synchronically or diachronically? The only absolute rule is that the interpretation we arrive at cannot violate our antecedent understanding of the poem.

This relationship of literary understanding and interpretation suggests that the same process must obtain for all humanistic understanding and interpretation—for the understanding and interpretation of paintings, houses, campaign speeches, experiments in molecular biology, editorials, and sermons. Together all these documents constitute the particular form of culture that concerns the humanist. The system whereby we understand poems intrinsically is called the theory of literature. Accordingly, there must be something analogous to that theory—insofar as humanistic studies are concerned—for these other kinds of documents. Such understanding must be prior to interpretation, of whatever scope. The humanistic understanding of an experiment in molecular biology would not aim at comprehending the place of the experiment in a series of such experiments, leading to increasingly correct knowledge of the problem. Rather, it would aim at comprehending the experiment—through understanding—as an exemplum of *gesta humanorum*, an abidingly powerful and significant instance of man's attempt to discover humanity not only in his world, but also in himself. Interpretation would follow and would yield a specifically humanistic history of science.[4] This would also be true, I think, for the humanistic mode of understanding and interpreting other kinds of documents.

3

The documents that humanists study have a certain prestige and privilege. They are "expressive" in the fullest sense. Thus Robert Redfield has pointed out:

4. A detailed exposition of a mode in the history of science somewhat analogous to the one I have designated here is Gerald Holton, "The Thematic Imagination in Science," in G. Holton, ed., *Science and Culture* (Boston: Houghton Mifflin Company, 1965), pp. 88-108.

Both humanist and social scientist have access, through the study of materials both different and similar, to the systems of values that distinguish humanity.

To study states of mind, we need expressive documents. Whether we undertake the study of humanity as a student of the arts and of literature or as a social scientist, we find or we make expressive documents. The materials of social science and of the humanities are essentially the same. A tool is expressive in that it shows the purpose of the user and perhaps something of the skill of the maker. In so far as it is a work of fine art, it shows something still more significant: something of the standards of technical performance and perhaps of aesthetic satisfaction. A personal letter is in many cases more richly expressive than a tool; and a curse, a chance remark, a word said in passion, a folk tale and a novel—these are very expressive indeed.[5]

Further, such documents are expressive of man's possibilities for making history, even as it has made him. In the words of Américo Castro:

History is where are realized, in many ways, man's possibilities for achieving great deeds and works that endure and radiate their values afield, works that effectively quicken and make fruitful in other men the capacity for reasoning and the longing to break out of the common round of daily insignificance, in other words, that can affect the mind, the imagination, or the soul.[6]

The humanist's task is, of course, to identify such documents, giving them prestige and privilege only when they satisfy the kind of criteria that Redfield and Castro delineate. These documents have an "overplus" of value. They not only serve their primary and initial function, but are also expressive and symbolic of the special values of their kind taken as a class. They are quite literally central, having accrued to themselves the aims, aspirations, functions, and even the style of the documentary mode that they express. What is said of one kind of such documents, poems (I mean poems that matter to us), can be said of all: Crucial to their centrality are special languages (or whatever media appropriate) that call attention to themselves. In their origin, perhaps, their special value accrues from the powerful expression of quite prag-

5. Robert Redfield, "Social Science Among the Humanities," *Human Nature and the Study of Society* (Chicago: University of Chicago Press, 1962), pp. 49-50.

6. Américo Castro, *The Structure of Spanish History* (Princeton: Princeton University Press, 1954), p. 31.

matic functions. But, as the humanist sees *ex post facto*, they have *appreci-ated* in historical fact and have added significantly to man's sense of himself. Granting them prestige and privilege, we try to understand and then interpret them. We would endeavor to comprehend their principle of expression, a compound of their functioning as forms of discourse (as paintings, houses, poems, campaign speeches, experiments in molecular biology, editorials, or sermons) and as centrally symbolic vehicles for that aspect of human aspiration their forms of discourse represent. We would know documents as deeds—*gesta humanorum*.

4

I can put my generalizing remarks into proper perspective by considering what for an Americanist like me is one of the principal works of humanistic scholarship of our time, Henry Nash Smith's *Virgin Land: The American West as Symbol and Myth*.[7] Beyond its major contribution to our substantive understanding of its subject, *Virgin Land* is a basic document in the humanistic studies, precisely because the criteria of its inquiry are as various as its materials. The logic of its structure suggests how it articulates in great detail some of the problems of humanistic studies. In looking at the dialectic and not the history of its composition, I am concerned with logical and structural priorities and relationships and with how the book directs us to make up our minds, not with how Professor Smith makes up his mind. Perhaps it is true that *le livre c'est l'homme même*, but in this case I for one am not competent to say so.

Everywhere in *Virgin Land* one can see how well Professor Smith has learned the lesson of A. O. Lovejoy's history of ideas. That lesson called for rigorously logical dissection as a first stage in the investigation into beliefs and the commitments and acts they entail. Late in his life Lovejoy said that he had come to believe that his work in the history of ideas was intended to make Wilhelm Dilthey possible. He meant by this that he wanted to cut through the foggy mystique of *Geistesgeschichte* to understand the elements that made up a given *Zeitgeist*. Thus, for Lovejoy the first stage was analytical and logical—the thinking through of the logical possibilities latent in any statement of belief or in any idea. His own

7. Henry Nash Smith, *Virgin Land: The American West as Symbol and Myth* (Cambridge: Harvard University Press, 1950).

best known work, of course, carried on this analytical mode, the mode of understanding, and he pursued relentlessly elements of a belief, an idea-complex, or a "philosophy" as they combined and recombined. What he seemed to discover were myriad paradoxes, since men are not necessarily logicians, except perhaps *ex post facto*. In a few essays, he went on to what he called the synthesizing stage of the historiography of ideas (the mode of interpretation): Combinations of unit ideas, however paradoxical or illogical they appeared, were placed in their sociocultural contexts and were shown as they shaped men's minds and opinions, leading them to act. These very acts led to new combinations of unit-ideas, new complexes, new commitments, and new acts.

I summarize Lovejoy's well-known method in order to point out that it also characterizes Professor Smith's book—latently, as it were. That is, I suspect that this initial analytic stage is not present in *Virgin Land* itself, but is antecedent to the book as Professor Smith wrote it for us. Note, for example, the paradoxically different views of the Western hero and of the West itself which Professor Smith details for us and the care with which he sets forth the strictly ideological elements of the paradox, even as he deals with its expressive elements. Further, the paradox, considered intellectually, is necessarily a logical one. Lovejoy's mode of thinking was the necessary condition of composing the book, even if it is not presented initially by way of a prolegomenon. This is worth pointing out, because it explains why and how Professor Smith has been able to break with the intellectual and cultural historians before him. They took the ideologies related to the West as given and then tried to place them in, derive them from, or relate them to their sociocultural contexts—or to see them as motivating agents. Indeed, *Virgin Land* is in part the history of histories of the West. It might well be that it was from this perspective that Professor Smith began his initial analysis. He concludes with an essay on the paradoxes on which Turner was hoist. I have a sense that, as a historian going to other historians, he makes his argument properly end where it has really begun.

Unhappily, Professor Smith says little about method. There is the teasingly modest statement in the preface:

> The terms "myth" and "symbol" occur so often in the following pages that the reader deserves some warning about them. I use the words to designate larger or smaller units of the same kind of thing, namely an intellectual construction that fuses concept and emotion into an image.

The myths and symbols with which I deal have the further characteristic of being collective representations rather than the work of a
single mind. I do not mean to raise the question whether such products
of the imagination accurately reflect empirical fact. They exist on a
different plane. But as I have tried to show, they sometimes exert a
decided influence on practical affairs.[8]

Professor Smith's conception of myth and symbol is made firm—and
more important, corrigible—by the necessary condition of Lovejoy's
"analytic" method. Moreover, the terms *myth* and *symbol* have, in
effect, little to do with the various kinds of mystiques—ranging from
non- to anti-historical—associated with their use in much contemporary literary criticism and philosophical anthropology and therefore said
to be "collective representations." But I find here none of the Jungian
(or pseudo- or quasi-Jungian) dogma of the archetype and its mysteries.
Nor, at the other extreme, do I find in Professor Smith's use of the terms
myth and *symbol* any of the socioeconomic reductionism of the sociology
of knowledge, pure or vulgar. *Myth* and *symbol* in *Virgin Land* are shown
to be collective representations: They embody ideas precisely as those
ideas are given shape and direction and are transformed into vital images
in the process—the quite empirically conceived historical process—of
"living" in the various sociocultural institutions in which Professor
Smith studies them and in the contexts of which he renders them. Their
forms follow their function at once as ideas and as vehicles for ideas.

Keeping this in mind, I find puzzling one sentence from the preface:
"I do not mean to raise the question whether such products of the
imaginations accurately reflect empirical fact." Professor Smith has, in
fact, continually raised this question—in his demystifying approach to
the matter of myth and symbol, in his concern to hold to the concept of
"intellectual construct," and in his analytic vigor. He means, I think,
that he will not act as *judge* of that segment of our past with which he
deals, but rather as *witness*. He will let us *see* the paradoxes and how they
emerge—how, in their paradoxical quality, they become images, and
distort, deny, or falsify empirical fact—and then he will let us do the
questioning. For surely we cannot help but ask questions, once we have
worked through *Virgin Land*.

In *Virgin Land*, Professor Smith implicates ideas in their sociocultural
contexts, thereby showing how images—myths and symbols—have

8. Ibid., p. vii.

developed. Our ability to ask valid questions depends on his success in this substantive core of the book. Let me cite a few examples.

In his treatment of the development of the Western hero, Leatherstocking and his personae, Professor Smith studies a highly institutionalized literary personage and the transformations worked on him by the pressures of literary conventions, the psychology of human behavior, the relationship between imagined and actual Westerners, the development of a mass audience, the technology whereby that development was forced, and the economics of publishing. Most important, I think, are the latter factors, involving the development of a mass audience. Professor Smith, in this instance, makes investigations at once qualitative and quantitative. The images developed and the congeries of myth and symbol are depicted as they take on institutional forms. Popular literature is treated in its true form, as the displacement of aesthetic structures by what are, in the end, predominantly or essentially economic structures. At one point by way of summary Professor Smith writes:

> Large-scale production implies regularity of output. The customer must be able to recognize the manufacturer's product by its uniform packaging—hence the various series [of Dime Novels] with their characteristic formats. But a standard label is not enough; the product itself must be uniform and dependable.[9]

At this stage Professor Smith is not discussing art per se, even popularized art per se, but art entirely implicated in economics. As the synthesizing intellectual and cultural historian must, he has not simply "placed" ideas in their sociocultural contexts, but has shown how those contexts create a special kind of image, to be understood, finally, as the product of the interaction of ideas and contexts. His word, following the argument of the preface, would be *fusion*. His subject at this point is not ideas, literary images, personae, or technology, but rather all of them at once as they are fused into one of the viable elements of that part of American sociocultural life vitally related to ideas of the West. Ideas are shown—to paraphrase Kenneth Burke—as they have become equipment for living. Through their expression in properly understood and interpreted documents, they are shown to be deeds—*gesta humanorum*.

Finding the right contexts for ideas, implicating as opposed to placing them in their contexts, and only then treating them as images—this

9. Ibid., p. 91.

is one of Professor Smith's great gifts, and a major contribution of *Virgin Land* to the technique (or the art) of humanistic studies. In the section entitled "Passage to India," the context is that of imperialist power politics. In the "Garden of the World," it is that of agrarian versus urban economic theorizing, the Free Soil issue, and utopian political theorizing. Without summarizing *Virgin Land*, I would only emphasize the way, in all cases, Professor Smith has taught us how to discover "collective representations"—fusions of concept and emotion—as the viable products of ideas implicated in empirically definable sociocultural institutions. Further, he has taught us to see that the resulting images carry with them the impression of the institutions involved, and so represent—however paradoxically when considered analytically—historical actuality, *our* historical actuality.

The fact that it is *our* historical actuality inevitably raises the question of the use, in particular, of *Virgin Land* and, in general, of its kind of intellectual history. I return to the statement of the preface: "I do not mean to raise the question whether such products of the imagination accurately reflect empirical fact." This might be Professor Smith's equivalent of Max Weber's famous reply to a question asking why he wrote the kind of historical sociology he did: "I wish to see how much I can bear." How can we treat sympathetically the follies and mistakes of our forebears, while yet declining to reduce them to a single master cause? How shall we carry out Professor Lovejoy's famous injunction:

> But though the history of ideas is a history of trial-and-error, even the errors illuminate the peculiar nature, the cravings, the endowments, and the limitations of the creature that falls into them, as well as the logic of the problems in reflection upon which they have arisen; and they may further serve to remind us that the ruling modes of thought of our own age, which some among us are prone to regard as clear and coherent and firmly grounded and final, are unlikely to appear in the eyes of posterity to have any of those attributes. The adequate record of even the confusions of our forebears may help, not only to clarify these confusions, but to engender a salutary doubt whether we are wholly immune from different but equally great confusions. For though we have more empirical information at our disposal, we have not different or better minds; and it is, after all, the action of the mind upon facts that makes both philosophy and science—and, indeed, largely makes the "facts."[10]

10. A. O. Lovejoy, *The Great Chain of Being* (Cambridge: Harvard University Press, 1936), p. 23.

Virgin Land calls for a position somewhat more "activist" than that demanded in *The Great Chain of Being*: The difference between a Lovejoy and a Smith as humanists is not only that between the analyst who would primarily understand and the synthesizer who would primarily interpret, but also that between the historian under the aegis of Zeus and the historian under the aegis of Prometheus. At one point Professor Smith writes: "These inferences from the myth of the garden will be recognized as the core of what we call isolationism."[11] This is not the statement of the historian who would teach us the lessons of the past or who would have us look down upon our forebears, even if the pure logic of our studies might permit. In context, it is the statement of a historian who conceives of intellectual and cultural history as a way of seizing directly the ideas that, as images in action, have helped form the decisions of our forebears and in part, therefore, those we make today. Such a historical work as *Virgin Land*, then, as it deals with "collective representations" is, in effect, collectively therapeutic. I am, of course, thinking of the psychoanalytic model—particularly of that model associated with ego-psychology: The patient gradually comes to grips with his past in all its paradoxes, confusions, and follies, and learns to accept it, to accept himself, and so perhaps to redirect himself, building his future more intelligently. Only if he accepts his past and knows it genuinely and authentically as his own can he be free. And this is precisely the desired effect of the work of the humanist as witness.

Whereas intellectual history in the analytic sense gives us comprehension, in the synthetic sense (the sense of *Virgin Land*) it gives us insight. Comprehension, of course, in the process of psychoanalytic therapy seems to be a precondition of insight. Comprehension sorts things out and places them; insight puts them together and implicates them in the deep biography that is the history of the patient. A similar process, I think, at the level of "collective representation" is at work in *Virgin Land*. Professor Smith seems in significant part to have anticipated the question raised in 1962 by Erik Erikson:

> The question is whether the historian and psychoanalyst can bridge the gap between psychic reality and historical actuality and discern together, not only whether and why a leader's or a people's opinions and actions seem irrational from a rationalist's point of view, but also

11. Smith, *Virgin Land*, p. 188.

what alternatives are most acute in historical actuality; not only what apprehensions seem to endanger, but also what opportunities seem to promise a more inclusive sense of identity and security. For collective as well as individual adaptation is furthered only by the proper ratio of insight offered and of action "sponsored."[12]

Virgin Land is a rational book dealing sympathetically with the irrational. It treats of "alternatives . . . most acute in historical actuality," "apprehensions," and "opportunities," because in their various socioculturally conditioned forms they were immediately present to those whose alternatives, apprehensions, and opportunities they actually were. The questions required deal with our relationship to these possibilities and their analogues in our time and must be asked in all the variegated forms and structures of the language of those for whom the questions first arose, those who first answered them, however wisely or foolishly. The dialectic of *Virgin Land* lets us see that those answers were originally questions and, further, helps explain how, why, and to what purpose they arose. In the end one does not question the world of *Virgin Land*; one is questioned by it. As the myths and symbols of *Virgin Land*—to use Erikson's terms—have "sponsored" the actions of its protagonists, so they give us insight into them and into ourselves since we can acknowledge them as our forebears and progenitors.

5

Virgin Land goes far; the humanist's professional utopianism, however, bids him declare that it could go further. Most of all, a clearer differentiation is needed between the antebellum American's sense of his human nature as against Henry Nash Smith's sense of that nature. In *Virgin Land* there is a slight tendency to psychologize after the fact—to interpret a man like Cooper, for example, as being a kind of split personality. He is seen as somehow secretly longing for the primitivistic world of Leatherstocking, when in fact he worked out a scheme whereby he demonstrated to himself (consciously at least) that such a world was lost and gone forever, a price paid for the high world of civilization that had succeeded it. Professor Smith's mode of implication, his deployment of the concepts of myth and symbol, does not sufficiently take into

12. Erik Erikson, "Psychological Reality and Historical Actuality," *Insight and Responsibility* (New York: Norton, 1964), p. 215.

account that most vexatious problem of change in concepts of human nature.

This, then, is for humanistic interpretation the abiding problem that modes of implication pose for us. The modes center on synthesizing terms like idea, idea-complex, ideology, structure, genre, theme, icon, metaphor, myth, style, poetics, symbol, national character, and the like. Such terms exist at different levels of abstraction, since they more or less include aspects of the expressive documents they enable us to relate to each other as well as to the cultures out of which they come and to our own. Moreover, such terms represent our retrospective interrelating of expressive (or privileged) documents, of the conscious and deliberate notion of members of the culture, or of both. Such distinctions are not crucial so long as we make the proper discriminations—not imputing a conscious use of a synthesizing term where factually it would be an error. It is crucial that we realize what is entailed in our use of such synthesizing terms and then act on that realization.

These terms are *normative*, precisely because they help us discover a principle of coherence among the documents they enable us to interrelate and because that principle itself derives from a culture's sense of its own coherence. This coherence principle, it seems to me, always involves two elements—a theory of human nature and a theory of society. Functionally, the two constitute a single principle.

Thus the poetics of Aristotle (in his *Poetics* and elsewhere), Sidney, Shelley, Lessing, Croce, and Jakobson set forth what poetry is or should be according to the theorist's sense of the self, society, and their interrelations. These interrelations, whether set forth explicitly or implicitly, must be taken into account if we are to understand a given system of poetics as a factor enabling us to implicate poems in their culture. Moreover, each student of these poems—privileged expressive documents— has his own conception of poetics, tied to his own sense of the self, society, and their interrelations. As interpreter, he seeks to find such congruence as there is between *his* poetics (likely to be that of his culture) and that of Aristotle and others. There will surely be congruence, to the degree that there appear to be "universals" in the self, society, and their interrelations.[13] The fact of congruence makes for the continuity of one expressive document—indeed, of one culture—to

13. Cf. Robert Redfield, "The Universally Human and the Culturally Variable," *Human Nature*, pp. 439-52, and the essay by Erikson cited above.

another and so permits understanding and interpretation. The fact of congruence, moreover, makes possible our implicating a poem at once in its own culture and in ours. The *quality* of implication will differ; comprehending such differences is the essence of humanistic studies. The fact of congruence enables us to recognize and take pleasure in the difference. We will, if skilled enough, learn even to interpret our poetics (and the poems whose qualities it prescribes) in the light of that of another culture, just as at the same time we interpret the poetics (and poems) of another culture in the light of our own. That is to say, the proper use of synthesizing terms like *poetics* can lead us to the enhancement of the humanist's proper sense of the plenitude of cultures and the possibilities for "authenticity" that their expressive documents demonstrate they offer.

I have instanced here only the case of poetics as a synthesizing term, but a similar case could be made for other terms. My main concern has been to suggest why, how, and to what end such terms are normative. Centrally involved is the need for all humanists to attend more closely to the theories of human nature and society that set the norms that bind such synthesizing terms as well as the expressive documents they synthesize. The normative quality of such terms gives them their distinct worth in humanistic studies, for that quality leads to the study of values, modes of valuation, affects, and *Erlebnis*; studying expressiveness itself leads us to that *critical involvement* which is our professional charge. If through the use of such synthesizing terms we are enabled to implicate expressive documents in their cultures, then perforce we are implicated ourselves—and as writers and teachers, we can implicate others. *Critical involvement* thus yields *judicial implication*. A given poetics is tied to a given theory of human nature and a given theory of society, as are the poems it would enable us to implicate in their culture and ours. And we can judge—we must judge—the degree to which a given theory of human nature and a given theory of society manifest, in the expressive documents as we can implicate them in their culture, enable (or disable) that full and free realization of human potentiality in society which is our abiding concern as humanists. The theory of human nature and society—a theory as it is a variant of that *central* theory which we continually must seek—is at the heart of the idea of the dignity of man.

As humanists we are interested in what man has achieved in the light of what he might have achieved. Thus we construct our critiques of societies and cultures by understanding and interpreting privileged documents as expressive of *gesta humanorum*. The documents project deeds done on behalf of man, although often in spite of man. Within the terms of this inevitable paradox is played out man's aspiration to dignity—which must be, we now see, at once individual and collective. The humanist understands human nature, at once deriving from culture and adding to it, as it achieves its characteristic expressions—in documents central to those expressions, *gesta humanorum*. If we have the means to understand documents and the modes to interpret them—and also a sufficiently open and flexible sense of the nature of the men whose deeds they express and of the possibilities and impossibilities for human dignity—we shall be in that position, at once humbling and ennobling, which Emerson described in his essay, "History":

> We sympathize in the great moments of history, in the great discoveries, the great resistances, the great prosperities of men; because law was enacted, the sea was searched, the land was found, or the blow was struck, *for us*, as we ourselves in that place would have done or applauded.

1970

2

POETRY AND PROGRESS/
CRITICISM AND CULMINATION:
A POLEMICAL POSTSCRIPT BY WAY
OF A CAUTIONARY TALE

1

My role as the teller of this tale is that of a historian of ideas in the Lovejovian mode—that in which I was long ago trained. It will be recalled that the moral of virtually all of Lovejoy's tales is that, properly viewed *ex post facto*, the beliefs and commitments (which together constitute what Lovejoy called "ideas" and "idea complexes") of our ancestors may appear not at all ridiculous if understood in their developing intellectual and sociocultural contexts; that, moreover, we might become somewhat self-consciously critical of our own beliefs and commitments (to the point that we might recognize their potential for the ridiculous) through the properly carried-out exercise of relating them in their continuity to those of our ancestors. Lovejoy felt that among his principal "foes" were those *esprits simplistes* who as progressivists were either self-congratulatory or self-flagellating—that is, those who would assure themselves that they were either the heritors or the victims of an ineluctable idea of progress. This then will be a Lovejovian exercise— with I hope that proper component of irony deriving from a post-Lovejovian's abiding and compulsive sense of human limitation: a sense of the human project as being gloriously tragicomical.

Thus an epigraph is called for. It follows, Kenneth Burke's poem, "Creation Myth":

> In the beginning, there was universal Nothing.
> Then Nothing said No to itself and thereby begat Something.
> Which called itself Yes.
>
> Then No and Yes, cohabiting, begat Maybe.

19

Next all three, in a ménage à trois, begat Guilt.
And Guilt was of many names:
Mine, Thine, Yours, Ours, His, Hers, Its, Theirs—and Order.

In time things so came to pass
That two of its names, Guilt and Order,
Honoring their great progenitors, Yes, No, and Maybe,
Begat History.

Finally, History fell a-dreaming
And dreamed about Language—

(And that brings us to critics-who-write-critiques-of-
        critical-criticism.)

2

    Among those whose researches and speculations have led them to
conclude that historical process is necessarily progressive, as though it
were the result of a "law," there is an overwhelming tendency, as
regards poetry (indeed, the arts in general), to come to primitivistic or
utopian conclusions. That is to say, they conclude that poetry (here let
"poetry" stand for "literature") was necessarily at its best and most
powerful in a time now past, under sociocultural conditions less complex than those that now obtain; or they conclude that poetry will
necessarily be at its best and most powerful at some time in the future,
under sociocultural conditions more complex than those that now
obtain. The speculative historians to whom I refer, let it be said at the
outset, were for the most part not primarily concerned with or interested in poetry. They were if at all only incidentally literary critics or
historians. Rather, their concern was, in the process of designing a
theory of historical development as a mode of progress, to place human
institutions—among them poetry in its making—in that development.
I want here to instance some key examples of both the primitivistic and
the utopian aspects of their researches and speculations and then briefly
to inquire into the bearing that all of this might have for our present
understanding of poetry and the criticism that it entails.

    Although there are adumbrations of these notions in classical, medi-
eval, and renaissance thought, it is during the Enlightenment that they
begin to take definitive shape. With the coming of the four-stage theory of sociocultural development, particularly in the so called Scottish
Enlightenment, the problem of literature as an institution is systemat-

ically confronted. That theory, to summarize it, held that inevitably society goes through stages of development that are tied to modes of subsistence and that social and cultural institutions are to be comprehended precisely as effects and outcomes of those modes: hunting, pastoral, agricultural, and commercial—to use the favored terms. Movement from one mode to another was taken to be necessary and for the good, thus progressive. There were institutions specific to each stage of development, and each of these institutions had virtues integral to it. But the *kinds* of virtues specific to each stage had become progressively better, since complementary to the stage-specific virtues were necessary (because also stage-specific) weaknesses and faults. Thus in the earlier stages men, because of the institutional structure of their society, would be particularly courageous, marked above all by personal bravery; and their interpersonal relations would be especially close and spontaneous. On the other hand, at these earlier stages, men would necessarily be cruel, given to warfare; their religion would not be "refined"; they would be incapable of that kind of abstract thinking which made for true philosophizing, higher learning. These latter qualities and capacities of course derived from the institutional structure of societies in the later stages of development, particularly the late agricultural and the commercial stages. There would be no blinking the fact that much had been lost; yet much more had been gained. Among the things that had been lost—necessarily lost—was the capacity to make great poetry.

Adam Ferguson perhaps best sums up this primitivistic view in his *Essay on the History of Civil Society* (1767). Having at length demonstrated that it is man's sociocultural institutions which, as they have derived from developing modes of subsistence, have on the whole improved, he goes on freely to admit that man at the earlier stages of his development produces the best poetry:

> Under the supposed disadvantage of a limited knowledge, and a rude apprehension, the simple poet has impressions that more than compensate the defects of his skill. The best subjects of poetry, the characters of the violent and the brave, the generous and the intrepid, great dangers, trials of fortitude and fidelity, are exhibited within his view, or are delivered in traditions which animate like truth, because they are equally believed. He is not engaged in recalling, like Virgil or Tasso, the sentiments or scenery of an age remote from his own; he needs not be

told by the critic, to recollect what another would have thought, or in what manner another would have expressed his conception. The simple passions, friendship, resentment, and love, are the movements of his own mind, and he has no occasion to copy.[1]

There is, I emphasize, no desire on Ferguson's part—nor on that of those of his peers of whom I make him exemplary—to return to that stage of society, and to its institutions, which has made great poetry directly (that is, most powerfully) possible. Writing of that "barbarian" poet Homer in 1735, another Scot, Thomas Blackwell, put the matter succinctly when he expressed, as he put it, his "Wish . . . *That we may never be a proper subject of an Heroic poem.*"[2]

This of course is not the occasion to anthologize such views. Hence I merely instance, in addition to the Scots, Vico, Turgot, Hazlitt, among others, as being, so far as poetry is concerned, primitivists by virtue of being progressivists. But I must cite one other famous instance of a thinker, committed to a theory of historical process at once progressivist and inevitablist, who, for all his admitted sophistication in literary matters, held to the primitivistic view:

A man cannot become a child again, or he becomes childish. But does he not find joy in the child's naïveté, and must he himself not strive to reproduce its truth at a higher stage? Does not the true character of each epoch come alive in the nature of its children? Why should not the historic childhood of humanity, its most beautiful unfolding, as a stage never to return, exercise an eternal charm? There are unruly children and precocious children. Many of the old peoples belong in this category. The Greeks were not normal children. The charm of their art for us is not in contradiction to an undeveloped stage of society on which it grew. [It] is its result, rather, and is inextricably bound up, rather, with the fact that the unripe social conditions under which it arose, and could alone rise, can never return.[3]

This of course is Marx, in the *Grundrisse* (1857). So much then for my first set of examples of the progressivist as, so far as poetry is concerned, the primitivist.

1. Adam Ferguson, *Essay on the History of Civil Society* (1767; rpt. Edinburgh: Edinburgh University Press, 1966), p. 173.
2. Thomas Blackwell, *An Enquiry into the Life and Writings of Homer* (London: n.p., 1735), p. 28.
3. Karl Marx, *Grundrisse*, rpt. trans. Martin Nicolaus (1857; rpt. New York: Random House, 1973), p. 11.

The utopian view occurs as early as Condorcet's *Sketch for a Historical Picture of the Progress of the Human Mind* (circa 1794). And it occurs in Mill's *System of Logic* (1843). Precisely because it is utopian, it is too generalized to get at in and of itself; for it must exist only as part of a desiderated system. Great poetry will come, we are told. But at this stage, its specific nature and quality can only be generally postulated. What is important for us, in the context of our immediate concerns, is that great poetry—or perhaps one should say, the greatest poetry—cannot be admitted to exist now or to have existed in the past. Thus another progressivist as utopian, Comte, in the *Cours de Philosophie Positive* (1830-1842):

> For five centuries, society has been seeking an aesthetic constitution correspondent to its civilization. In the time to come—apart from all consideration of the genius that will arise, which is wholly out of the reach of anticipation—we may see how art must eminently fulfill its chief service, of charming and improving the humblest and the loftiest minds, elevating the one and soothing the other. For this service it must gain much by being fitly incorporated with the social economy, from which it has hitherto been essentially excluded. . . . The most original and popular species of modern art, which forms a preparation for that which is to ensue, has treated of private life, for want of material in public life. But public life will be such as will admit of idealization, for the sense of the good and the true cannot be actively conspicuous without eliciting a sense of the beautiful, and the action of the positive philosophy is in the highest degree favorable to all three. The systematic regeneration of human conceptions must also furnish new philosophical means of aesthetic expansion, secure at once of a noble aim and a steady impulsion. There must certainly be an inexhaustible resource of poetic greatness in the positive conception of man as the supreme head of the economy of nature, which he modifies at will in a spirit of boldness and freedom, within no other limits than those of natural law. . . . What philosophy elaborates, art will propagate and adapt for propagation, and will thus fulfill a higher social office than in its most glorious days of old.[4]

Reading such generalized prose (as R. P. Blackmur said on a corresponding occasion) is like punching a mattress. And I find that I don't get much further when I try to read the utopian remarks about poetry

---

4. Auguste Comte, *Cours de Philosophie Positive*, 6 vols., trans. Harriet Martineau (1830-1842; rpt. London: John Champman, 1953), 2:559-60.

by more recent committed progressivists—specifically Marxists ranging from Trotzky to Marcuse. But that doesn't particularly matter here,
since my concern is simply to indicate notions of the fate of poetry and
the criticism it entails as they are considered by ideologues of progress
when they are either in a primitivistic or a utopian mood.

3

I come then to some recent examples. I wish that I could quote them
without attribution, since I want to take them as ideal-typical
expressions of their sentiments. Let them be at least documents nearly
anonymous.

There has developed over the past fifteen years or so a literary movement called ethnopoetics. Its primary impulse is somehow to "recover"
those oral—not by any means "primitive"—poetries which, even if
they have been put on the written record, have become aesthetically lost
to us. Or rather, so the argument goes (and I am persuaded by it), to our
own impoverishment, we have become lost to them. The movement is,
for me, a most important one. It has resulted in the recovery and reex-
amination of many, many texts, the taping of contemporary oral poetries in the field, new modes of exegesis and, more important,
translation, and also consideration of the problem of orality itself. Inevitably, since much of the material involved comes from the so-called
Third World, Marxist critics, with all their progressivist commitments, have dealt with these poetries and have involved themselves in
the ethnopoetic movement. Quite naturally indeed, they have tried to
define it. A few years ago, there was held a large-scale conference on
ethnopoetics, and some of the papers there delivered were subsequently
published in *Alcheringa*, then the movement's main journal.

One of the papers, claiming that the name of the movement should
be *socio*poetics, gives this primitivistic account of the place these poetries
should play in our lives. (The quotation marks, italics, and capitals are
in the original):

> As western man "pacified" New World nature, eliminated the "sav-
> age," penned them up in reservations, he did the same with whole areas
> of his Being. Indeed, it would be difficult to explain the extraordinary
> nature of his (imperialist) ferocity if we did not see that it was, first of
> all, a ferocity also wrought, in psychic terms, upon himself. Western
> man—as defined by the bourgeoisie—restrained those areas of Being

whose *mode of knowing* could sustain the narrative conceptualiza-
tion . . . of his new world picture, but eliminated, penned up on reser-
vations—those areas of *cognition* which were, by their mode of
knowing, *heretical* to the conceptualized orthodoxy that was required.
THE MODE OF COGNITION THAT WAS PENNED UP WAS A
MODE WHICH WESTERN MAN (ALL OF US, SINCE IT IS NO
LONGER A RACIAL BUT A CULTURAL TERM) REMAINS
AWARE OF ONLY THROUGH POETRY—AND POETRY AS
THE GENERIC TERM FOR ART.

Thus the primitivistic view of poetry by a progressivist critic, which, if
only we allow for differences in rhetoric, has a distinct affiliation with
Ferguson's "the simple passions, friendship, resentment, and love, are
the movements of his own mind, and he has no occasion to copy."

But this progressivist's view is also utopian. For she continues immediately:

> HENCE IT WOULD SEEM TO ME TO BE THE POINT OF
> THIS CONFERENCE: THE EXPLORATION OF THIS *ALTER-
> NATIVE MODE OF COGNITION* IDEOLOGICALLY SUP-
> PRESSED IN OURSELVES, YET STILL A LIVING FORCE
> AMIDST LARGE MAJORITIES OF THE THIRD WORLD PEO-
> PLES. IN THIS COMMON EXPLORATION THERE CAN
> THEN BE NO CONCEPT OF A LIBERAL MISSION TO SAVE
> "PRIMITIVE POETICS" FOR "PRIMITIVE PEOPLES." THE
> SALVAGING OF OURSELVES, THE RECLAMATION OF VAST
> AREAS OF OUR BEING, IS DIALECTICALLY RELATED TO
> THE DESTRUCTION OF THOSE CONDITIONS WHICH
> BLOCK THE FREE DEVELOPMENT OF THE HUMAN
> POTENTIALITIES OF THE MAJORITY PEOPLES OF THE
> THIRD WORLD.[5]

A commenter on this paper sums it up, putting the matter in perspective:

> So it is important, that after all of that individualistic lyricism there
> should finally emerge a lyric production that reasserts its links to the
> mainstream of art in human societies, and attempts to reinvent that
> social and collective function which poetry and the changed or spoken
> or sung have had over all but the most recent centuries of human his-
> tory.[6]

5. Sylvia Winter, "Ethno or Socio Poetics," *Alcheringa*, n.s. 2 (1976):83.
6. Fredric Jameson, "Collective Art in the Age of Cultural Imperialism,"
Alcheringa, n.s. 2 (1976):108.

Another primitivist example is perhaps somewhat more sophisticated than the one I have just instanced. Lukács's *Theory of the Novel* has proved somewhat difficult for Marxist critics precisely because it is not one of Lukács's specifically Marxist treatises. I quote the summarizing bit of a recent (I take it) Marxist resolution of this difficulty. What is centrally at issue is Lukács's understanding of "realism":

> If Lukács' theory of representation is "dogmatic" and reductive of the complexity of history and the novel, this "dogmatism" does not really "originate" in his concept of "historicity" in *The Theory of the Novel* . . . , nor with his conversion to Marxism. . . . Rather the ideal, harmonious presence he attributes to the origin of history in Greece dominates, though not simply and without contradiction, both his early "pre-Marxist," "idealist" work and his later "Marxist," "materialistic" work. The origin of history is never really "lost" for Lukács; for representation is the dialectic at work in fiction to ensure that the presence of harmonious man, that "his" poetry, will be conserved and projected forward onto the end of history. To transform a phrase of Lukács from *The Theory of the Novel*, in this view of history, the historical journey is over as soon as the voyage begins. The presence of harmonious man as the essence of all representation (and interpretation) has put an end to the conflicts, contradictions, and differences of history. Representation in this abstract, dialectical sense *is* the end or the elimination of history.[7]

Only recall the passage from Marx I have already quoted. What is happening here is an appeal (dialectical in good part, as in the statements I have previously quoted, via the diacritical marks) to that idea of Gemeinschaft—the primitivist—which is of course at the heart of the passage from Marx: Greek society was genuinely communitarian; modern society is not, but could be; poetry is possible only in a Gemeinschaftlich society. Lukács's notion of realism and the novel can be understood as deriving from a desiderated Gemeinschaft precisely as the novel is the modern analogue of the epic. Thus Lukács is even at this stage taken to be a Marxist in spite of himself—and I would add, necessarily a primitivist. The open question remains: Does "the end or the elimination of history" entail the end or the elimination of poetry, of literature? Just as we may devoutly hope that we may never be the subjects of heroic poems, should we hope that we may never be the

7. David Carroll, "Representation or the End(s) of History: Dialectics and Fiction," *Yale French Studies* 59 (1980):228-29.

subjects of novels?—the subjects of history? Indeed, can we hope that we may not in any event be *subjects*?

Now for some examples of the progressivist as utopian. Here, I must point out, it develops that we are confronted by a criticism that, having its way with poetry, is culminating. I give three examples, all in the mode we have been instructed to call structuralist, or post-structuralist, or post-post-structuralist:

> There are thus two interpretations of interpretation, of structure of sign, of freeplay. The one seeks to decipher, dreams of decipherment, a truth or an origin which is free from freeplay and from the order of the sign, and lives like an exile the necessity of interpretation. The other, which is no longer turned toward the origin, affirms freeplay and tries to pass beyond man and humanism, the name being the name of that being who, throughout the history of metaphysics and of onto-theology—in other words, through the history of all of his history—has dreamed of full presence, the reassuring foundation, the origin and end of the game.[8]

> There is therefore in every present mode of writing a double postulation: there is the very shape of every revolutionary situation, the fundamental ambiguity of which is that Revolution must of necessity borrow, from what it wants to destroy, the very image of what it wants to possess. Like modern art in its entirety, literary writing carries at the same time the alienation of History and the dream of History; as a Necessity, it testifies to the division of languages which is inseparable from the division and the very effort which seeks to surmount it. Feeling permanently guilty of its own solitude, it is none the less an imagination eagerly desiring a felicity of words, it hastens towards a dreamed-of language whose freshness, by a kind of ideal anticipation, might portray the perfection of some new Adamic world where language would no longer be alienated. The proliferation of modes of writing brings a new Literature into being in so far as the latter invents its language only in order to be a project: Literature becomes the Utopia of language.[9]

This suggests one final approach to the Text, that of pleasure. I do not know if a hedonistic aesthetic ever existed, but there certainly exists

8. Jacques Derrida, "Structure, Sign, and Play," in *The Structuralist Controversy*, ed. R. Macksey and E. Donato (Baltimore: Johns Hopkins University Press, 1970), pp. 264-65.

9. Roland Barthes, *Writing Degree Zero*, trans. Annette Lavers and Colin Smith (1953; rpt. London: Jonathan Cape, 1967), pp. 93-94.

a pleasure associated with the work (at least with certain works). I can enjoy reading and rereading Proust, Flaubert, Balzac, and even—why not?—Alexandre Dumas; but this pleasure, as keen as it may be and even if disengaged from all prejudice, remains partly (unless there has been an exceptional critical effort) a pleasure of consumption. If I can read those authors, I also know that I cannot *rewrite* them (that today, one can no longer write "like that"); that rather depressing knowledge is enough to separate one from the production of those works at the very moment when their remoteness founds one's modernity (for what is "being modern" but the full realization that one cannot begin to write the same works once again). The Text, on the other hand, is linked to enjoyment, to pleasure without separation. Order of the signifier, the Text participates in a social utopia of its own; prior to history, the Text achieves, if not the transparency of social relations, at least the transparency of language relations. It is the space in which no one language has a hold over any other, in which all languages circulate freely.[10]

Were these last three texts taken from a dialogue by Sir Thomas More, I could come directly to grips with them. As it is, I must come indirectly, noting that they seem to be claiming that, once a text is freed from its context (in the language of the last, once a "work" is taken as a "text"), the critic achieves a certain utopian freedom to do as he is pleasured to do, not as the text wills him (often to his displeasure) to do. The subject-object problem at the heart of Western metaphysics and ontology ("onto-theology"?), thus at the heart of Western criticism, is solved by the elimination (or repression) of the object—this under the guise of getting rid of the bothersome existence of the subject. The critical mode culminates as the critic becomes not the inventor but rather the creator of all he surveys. As with neo-Marxist primitivism, structuralist utopianism issues into a hope for the withering away of literature, as literature no longer consists of more or less stable works by more or less unstable writers but of texts that occasion the celebration of the stability of readers—the role of criticism itself about to wither away.

4

There is, I think, a lesson (or moral) for us in this tale—however foreshortened my telling it has been. I noted at the outset that there was

10. Barthes, "From Work to Text," in *Textual Strategies*, trans. Josué V. Harrari (1971; rpt. Ithaca: Cornell University Press, 1979), pp. 80-81.

a "tendency" in the progressivist writers whom I have instanced to come to primitivistic or utopian conclusions. Let me change "tendency" to "temptation"—and add that the "temptation" has been "yielded to." The temptation derives, I think, from an insistence, an assumption transformed into a principle, that history has a plot. And if there is a plot, there must of course be a beginning, middle, and something corresponding to an end—not to say a series of denouements. Poetry, according to this line of argument, like other sociocultural institutions, must not only be related to and/or derived from collective activities, it must itself be at base a collective activity, an activity whose development can as such be "plotted." And in seeking out evidence of that collective activity and of its plotting, the progressivist historian perforce in good part blinds himself to the fact that poetry is made up of poems *qua* poems, of individual statements that, however much they respond to collectively developed modes of expression (literary "conventions" or, more fashionably, "mediations") remain nonetheless individual. I note that in the first place, reading poems (and I daresay, making them), we are always in the middle, never at a beginning or an end. This is the existential fact that sets the historian of poetry his major problem of research, interpretation, and exposition. In the second place, the statements of which poems consist (or which poems make) are fictive—literature being that form of statement in which the capacity of language to make fictions is maximized. This in fact is poetry's— literature's—great use to us: that it allows us to explore to their uttermost *possible* implications the nature of our aspirations, beliefs, and commitments. It allows us indeed to explore them in a myriad series of alternate roles—as we can, in fictions, allow ourselves to imagine ourselves as being other than we are. The progressivist as primitivist or utopian, however can afford to believe only in the "real"—at most the probable, never the merely possible; his is the way of extrapolation, not imagination. Thus he must locate poetry at that stage in its history when it has appeared, or will appear, to be most real, not at all fictive— most identifiable with the sociocultural actualities in the context of which it has come into being. Since that stage, owing to the fictive nature of poetry, is never now, it must always have been or be yet to come. Thus necessarily poetry is discovered to be part and parcel of the collective plot of history.

I conclude—following the Lovejovian mode—that one test of the idea of progress is its use, as at least a heuristic device, in enabling us to come directly to grips with the objects (in this case poems) and the subjects (in this case poets and their readers) that constitute the matter it is to organize for us. And surely that idea, should we subscribe to it, would serve only to distance us from poetry and from ourselves as the subjects of poetry, from the very possibility of poetry, from the free and full employment of our knowledge of the languages and the institutions that condition poetry as a means of knowing ourselves for what we have been, what we are, what we might be. For even though, as I have outlined its various permutations, past and present, that idea is meant, as regards poetry, to describe the conditions of the making of poems, inevitably and necessarily it must prescribe the conditions of the reading of poems. In the case of poetry, the irony is that the idea of progress would confine and inhibit, not free, us—both as poets and as readers of poems. After all, primitivism and utopianism in the end as in the beginning derive from our constitutional fear of freedom within finitude. And freedom within finitude in the beginning as in the end constitutes the ultimate condition of poetry.

1983

II.

INTERPRETATIONS:
TOWARD UNDERSTANDING
AND BEYOND

After the final no there comes a yes
And on that yes the future world depends.
—Stevens, "The Well Dressed Man with a Beard"

3

POETRY, REVOLUTION,
AND THE AGE OF PAINE

1

In his middle age retired to Quincy, at once angry and meditative, John Adams wrote his good friend Benjamin Waterhouse, 29 October 1805, as follows:

> I am willing you should call this the Age of Frivolity as you do: and would not object if you had named it the Age of Folly, Vice, Frenzy, Fury, Brutality, Daemons, Buonaparte, Tom Paine, or the Age of Reason. I know not whether any Man in the World has had more influence on its inhabitants or affairs for the last thirty years than Tom Paine. There can be no severer Satyr on the Age. For such a mongrel between Pigg and Puppy, begotten by a wild Boar on a Bitch Wolf, never before in any Age of the World was suffered by the Poltroonery of mankind, to run through such a Career of Mischief. Call it then the Age of Paine.[1]

Adams, we can now say, protests too much. His own view of the causes, occasions, and ends of the Revolution, deriving from his whiggish conservatism, is directly expressive of his high-principled stubbornness, self-assurance, and agonizing sense that the Revolution had released forces (among them, Tom Paine) that were virtually beyond controlling. In spite of himself, as it were, he was caught up in the Age of Paine, his own moral and political ideology being just one variant of a larger, more inclusive, more complex, and internally contradictory ideology—that of the Revolution as an overwhelmingly accomplished fact: a fact, to use that terribly complicated enlightened word, of

1. W. C. Ford, ed., *Statesman and Friend: Correspondence of John Adams with Benjamin Waterhouse, 1784-1822* (Boston: Little, Brown and Co., 1927), p. 31.

Nature. That larger ideology subsumed its internal contradictions, and also the violence and dissension produced by those contradictions, in the notion that the Revolution itself was nothing if not eminently "reasonable"—the reason being that of Nature and Nature's God, fixed in the very structure of things, as Americans sought to design and to bring about the social, political, and economic arrangements that their sense of themselves in their world "naturally" demanded of them. Thus the thousands of pamphlets they wrote, from whatever "reasonable" perspective, conceived the Revolution as being above all "ideological." So powerful and telling was this "ideological" emphasis that it set the tone and style of interpretations of the Revolution through the end of the nineteenth century and beyond.

The great study of poetry in the American Revolution, Moses Coit Tyler's *Literary History of the American Revolution* (1897), is in this sense ideological.

> The same logic that drove the participants to view the Revolution as peculiarly intellectual also compelled Moses Coit Tyler, writing at the end of the nineteenth century, to describe the American Revolution as "preeminently a revolution caused by ideas, and pivoted on ideas." That ideas played a part in all revolutions Tyler readily admitted. But in most revolutions, like that of the French, ideas had been perceived and acted upon only when the social reality had caught up with them, only when the ideas had been given meaning and force by long-experienced "real evils." The American Revolution, said Tyler, had been different: it was directed "not against tyranny inflicted, but only against tyranny anticipated." The Americans revolted not out of actual suffering but out of reasoned principle. "Hence, more than with most other epochs of revolutionary strife, our epoch of revolutionary strife was a strife of ideas: a long warfare of political logic; a succession of annual campaigns in which the marshalling of arguments not only preceded the marshalling of armies, but often exceeded them in impression upon the final result."

I am quoting here from Gordon Wood's magisterial analysis of interpretations of the American Revolution.[2] He in turn is quoting from Tyler's *Literary History of the American Revolution*, which, as regards its study of revolutionary pamphleteering, has only relatively recently begun to be superseded and, as regards its analysis of revolutionary

2. "Rhetoric and Reality in the American Revolution," *William and Mary Quarterly*, ser. 3, 23 (1966):3-32. I quote from pp. 6-7.

poetry, drama, and fiction, has yet to be superseded. (One of my intentions in what follows is to suggest the direction that supersession might well take.) Professor Wood goes on in his analysis to review anti-ideological socioeconomic interpretations of the Revolutionary period as they occur in the work of Becker and Beard. But his principal concern is to deal with recent interpretations of the Revolution, his own and that of Perry Miller, Edmund Morgan, Bernard Bailyn, among others. He concludes that the Revolutionary period was indeed an Age of Paine, with Adams himself, beyond his own understanding, implicated in it, in all its painfulness. I quote Professor Wood again:

> When the ideas of the Americans are examined comprehensively, when all of the Whig rhetoric, irrational as well as rational, is taken into account, one cannot but be struck by the predominant characteristics of fear and frenzy, the exaggerations and the enthusiasm, the general sense of social corruption and disorder out of which would be born a new world of benevolence and harmony where Americans would become the "eminent examples of very divine and social virtue." As Bailyn and the propaganda studies have amply shown, there is simply too much fanatical and millennial thinking even by the best minds that must be explained before we can characterize the Americans' ideas as peculiarly rational and legalistic and thus view the Revolution as merely a conservative defense of constitutional liberties. To isolate refined and nicely-reasoned arguments from the writing of John Adams and Jefferson is not only to disregard the more inflamed expressions of the rest of the Whigs but also to overlook the enthusiastic extravagance—the paranoic obsession with a diabolical Crown conspiracy and the dream of a restored Saxon era—in the thinking of Adams and Jefferson themselves.
>
> The ideas of the American seem, in fact, to form what can only be called a revolutionary syndrome. . . . In the kinds of ideas expressed the American Revolution is remarkably similar to the seventeenth-century Puritan Revolution and to the eighteenth-century French Revolution: the same general disgust with a chaotic and corrupt world, the same anxious and angry bombast, the same excited fears of conspiracies by depraved men, the same utopian hopes for the construction of a new and virtuous order.[3]

With these last phrases Professor Wood might well be describing the poetry of the period—or rather, be describing it in its aspirations. For

3. Ibid., pp. 25-26.

disgust, anxiety, anger, fear, and hope do in fact constitute the tone of much of the poetry. But they are disgust, anxiety, anger, fear, and hope so compulsively projected outward, as part of the poets' commitment to *persuade* their readers, that they transform it altogether to rhetoric and so do not get absorbed and made constitutive of its integral quality. It is an overdetermined poetry. What we have, I think, is a case of poets, caught up in Revolutionary fervor, become idealogues, and so creating verse that is so much given over to its public function that we have little or no sense of the poet being—as he must be to be at his best—at once both a private and a public person. It is as though there were no *inside* to the Revolutionary experience, as though the poet himself, and thus his reader, were not somehow changed (for poetry at its best above all *changes* us) by his discovery and setting forth of his disgust, anxiety, fear, and hope. The historian of poetry—for that is what I am—would above all want his poets—for that is what they are—to be aware, in the very marrow of their being, that theirs was an Age of Paine. But, as I read them, they were not.

Surely, the *young* Freneau, writing collaboratively with his classmate at Princeton, Hugh Henry Brackenbridge, was not. I quote from the conclusion to their 1771 academic piece, "The Rising Glory of America":

> This is thy praise America thy pow'r
> Thou best of climes by science visited
> By freedom blest and richly stor'd with all
> The luxuries of life. Hail happy land
> The seat of empire the abode of kings,
> The final stage where time shall introduce
> Renowned characters, and glorious works
> Of high invention and wond'rous art,
> Which not the ravages of time shall waste
> Till he himself has run his long career;
> Till all those glorious orbs of light on high
> The rolling wonders that surround the ball,
> Drop from their spheres extinguish'd and consum'd;
> When final ruin with her fiery car
> Rides o'er creation, and all nature's works
> Are lost in chaos and the womb of night.

This is explicitly a public statement, so that we should accept at face value the ponderous blank verse and the simplistically overt diction. At *face* value, since there is little depth here. All is surface. Utopianism is pushed all the way, until there is even a withering away of poetry, or, rather, an advancement of poetry to rhetoric.

At the other extreme, there is the ballad and songwriting of the period. These are the third and fourth stanzas of an undated "American Soldier's Hymn":

> 'T is God that still supports our right,
> His just revenge our foes pursues;
> 'T is He that with resistless might,
> Fierce nations to His power subdues.
>
> Our universal safeguard He!
> From Whom our lasting honors flow;
> He made us great, and set us free
> From our remorseless bloody foe.

This is the opening stanza of "General Sullivan's Song," 1777:

> Hark, the loud drums, hark, the shrill trumpet-call to arms,
> Come, Americans come, prepare for war's alarms,
>   Whilst in array we stand,
>   What soldier dare to land,
>   Sure in the attempt to meet his doom,
>   A leaden death, or a watery tomb;
> We, Americans, so brave, o'er the land or the waves,
> All invaders defy, we'll repulse them or die,
>   We scorn to live as slaves.

And this is the beginning of "The Ballad of Nathan Hale," 1776:

> The breezes went steadily through the tall pines,
>   A-saying "oh! hu-ush!" a-saying "oh! hu-ush!"
> As stilly stole by a bold legion of horse,
>   For Hale in the bush, for Hale in the bush.
>
> "Keep still!" said the thrush as she nestled her young,
>   In a nest by the road; in a nest by the road.
> "For the tyrants are near, and with them appear
>   What bodes us no good, what bodes us no good."
>
> The brave captain heard it, and thought of his home
>   In a cot by the brook; in a cot by the brook.
> With mother and sister and memories dear,
>   He so gayly forsook; he so gayly forsook.

Perhaps it is necessary in the nature of songs and ballads to simplify, so to sharpen, the perceptions and understandings of their auditors. Perhaps in the long run it will be decided that indeed its songs and ballads are the most significant, or most typical, modes of verse of the Revolutionary period. My point is, however, that they too are essentially (again perhaps necessarily) rhetorical exercises. The examples of songs and ballads I have given—and there are, I emphasize, enough like these to make them typical—have this crucial quality in common with the bit from "The Rising Glory of America": they both derive from and are set in stock techniques and phrases—ranging from "elevated" blank verse and generalized figurative language to hymn- and ballad-style and language—such that, in employing an accepted and assured mode of expression, they may confirm and enforce their auditors' response and understanding. Auditors', really, in each case, not readers'. For these, and also the myriad others of their kind, are proclamatory poems, rhetorical verse, reaffirmations of shared, public commitments so clear and self-assured that their implications and entailments need not, cannot, be explored in that depth and subtlety which we know to characterize major—or serious—poetry. One of the most painful things—to those who witness it *ex post facto*—about an Age of Paine is that, for those who lived through it, its painfulness was comprehended and so transcended by its rectitude and its promise. This, I take it, is what issues when, in trying to witness and understand ourselves in our history, we put our rhetoric to the test of a poetry that could have been.

If, then, "The Rising Glory of America" represents public poetry— that is, poetry so overdetermined that it becomes rhetoric—at its most formal, and if the songs and ballads represent it at its most informal, the satirical verse of the period brings together the two modes and, in my opinion, is all the more effective for doing so.[4] There is an improvised, hard-hitting, journalistic verve in such satirical verse, both pro- and anti-Revolutionary. Moreover, there is a reliance on the technique of such verse in the British tradition, where the elegant and precise neo-classical mode had been transformed into a mode exuberantly inelegant and sweeping: the highest sort of journalism, one might say; a broad-sword instead of a rapier; rhetoric with a vengeance; sheer invective.

4. In the discussion of satire that follows I am of course principally indebted to the account, with its treasury of citations, given in Tyler's *Literary History of the American Revolution*. I have, however, gone to the original texts.

Thus an anonymous Loyalist satire on Tom Paine himself, published in the *New York Gazette*, 11 August 1779:

> Hail mighty Thomas! In whose works are seen
> A mangled Morris and a distorted Deane;
> Whose splendid periods flash for Lee's defense,—
> Replete with everything but Common Sense.
> You, by whose labors no man e'er was wiser,
> You, of invective great monopolizer;
> You, who, unfeeling as a Jew or Turk,
> Attack a Jay, a Paca, and a Burke;
> You, who, in fervor of satiric vein,
> Maul and abuse the mild and meek Duane,
> And eager to traduce the worthiest men,
> Despite the energy of Drayton's pen,—
> O say, what name shall dignify the lays
> Which now I consecrate to sing thy praise!
> In pity tell by what exalted name
> Thou would'st be damned to an eternal fame:
> Shall Common Sense, or Comus greet thine ear,
> A piddling poet, or puffed pamphleteer?

Thus, from the following year, the opening section of Jonathan Odell's Loyalist "The American Times":

> When Faction, pois'nous as the scorpion's sting,
> Infects the people and insults the King;
> When foul Sedition skulks no more conceal'd,
> But grasps the sword and rushes to the field;
> When Justice, Law, and Truth are in disgrace,
> And Treason, Fraud, and Murder fill their place;
> Smarting beneath accumulated woes,
> Shall we not dare the tyrants to expose?
> We will, we must—tho' mighty Laurens frown,
> Or Hancock with his rabble hunt us down;
> Champions of virtue, we'll alike disdain
> The guards of Washington, the lies of Payne;
> And greatly bear, without one anxious throb,
> The wrath of Congress, or its lords the mob.
> Bad are the Times, almost too bad to paint;
> The whole head sickens, the whole heart is faint;
> The State is rotten, rotten to the core,
> 'Tis all one bruize, one putrefying sore.

Here Anarchy before the gaping crowd
Proclaims the people's majesty aloud;
There folly runs with eagerness about,
And prompts the cheated populace to shout;
Here paper-dollars meagre Famine holds,
There votes of Congress Tyranny unfolds;
With doctrines strange in matter and in dress,
Here sounds the pulpit, and there groans the press;
Confusion blows her trump—and far and wide
The noise is heard—the plough is thrown aside;
The awl, the needle, and the shuttle drops;
Tools change to swords, and camps succeed to shops;
The doctor's glister-pipe, the lawyer's quill,
Transformed to guns, retain the power to kill;
From garrets, cellars, rushing thro' the street,
The new-born statesmen in committee meet;
Legions of senators infest the land,
And mushroom generals thick as mushrooms stand.

Odell, like the anonymous satirist I quoted before, of course goes on and on. Satire of this order becomes a litany of imprecation, without much structure or inclusive design or argument—no end envisaged because all is beginning. Fully felt, the pain of the Revolutionary situation is responded to and against, not understood. As in most cases of public poetry, who would be newly persuaded by satire such as this? In effect, the satire serves to confirm the opinion of a reader with Loyalist sympathies and so lets him assure himself that he is most surely at one with those with whose opinions he agrees. The satirist goes on and on, because if he talks long enough, he might postpone the inevitable.

So too with satire from the other side. I daresay *our* side. If it seems less assured than Loyalist satire, it is nonetheless as fully felt. ("Conservatives" seem always to have the best in satire.) This, for example, is a passage from Charles Henry Wharton's 1779 "A Poetical Epistle to George Washington, Esquire, Commander-in-Chief of the Armies of the United States of America"—the "Whitehead" mentioned in the fifth line being the then British Poet Laureate:

While many a servile Muse her succor lends
To flatter Tyrants, or a Tyrant's friends;
While thousands, slaughtered at Ambition's shrine
Are made a plea to court the tuneful Nine;

> Whilst Whitehead lifts his Hero to the skies,
> Foretells his conquests twice a year and lies,
> Damns half-starved Rebels to eternal shame,
> Or paints them trembling at Britannia's name;
> Permit an humble bard, great Chief, to raise
> One truth-erected trophy to thy praise.
> No abject flat'ry shall these numbers seek,
> To raise a blush on Virtue's modest cheek;
> Rehearse no merit, no illustrious deed,
> But Foes must own, & Washington may read.

The pro-Revolutionary satirist also so often seems to go on and on—at even greater length, I must say, than the Loyalist satirist. The best-known (because in its own time so widely publicized) of satires of this order is John Trumbull's *M'Fingal (1775-1782)*. Written in unintentionally clumsy Hudibrastics, overfull of intentional political, historical, classical, and literary allusions—thus more self-consciously "artful" than other satires of its time—it details the incapacity of its Tory hero to get anything right, even though at the end it envisages the victory of the side its hero opposes. Thus it celebrates inversely. As for satire—at one point a Whig crowd proceeds to tar and feather M'Fingal on a liberty pole:

> Forthwith the crowd proceed to deck
> With halter'd noose M'Fingal's neck,
> While he in peril of his soul
> Stood tied half-hanging to the pole;
> Then lifting high the ponderous jar,
> Pour'd o'er his head the smoking tar.
> With less profusion once was spread
> Oil on the Jewish monarch's head,
> That down his beard and vestments ran,
> And cover'd all his outward man.
> As when (so Claudian sings) the Gods
> And earth-born Giants fell at odds,
> The stout Enceladus in malice
> Tore mountaiuns up to throw at Pallas;
> And while he held them o'er his head,
> The river, from their mountains fed,
> Pour'd down his back its copious tide,
> And wore its channels in his hide;
> So from the high-raised urn the torrents
> Spread down his back their various currents. . . .

And so it goes, on and on, its mock-epic similes hunted out to the bitter end, as is M'Fingal himself. In this case, the satirist goes on and on because he would hasten the inevitable.

The problem for the Revolutionary satirist—one that accounts for his combining satire proper with argumentation—derived of course from his need to prove his own political position right while damning that of the opposition, whereas for the loyalist his political position was beyond need of being proved right. The loyalist can damn at will, whereas the Revolutionary must at once damn and argue, so as to celebrate.

The great example here of course is Philip Freneau. My subject as I have interpreted it lets me mention only in passing Freneau's capacity to be what used to be called a "pre-romantic" poet, with a sense of a natural world with which he would be at one and a sense of the constitutive power of the poetic fancy. (I think of course of poems like "The Beauties of Santa Cruz," "The Indian Burying Ground," "The Wild Honey Suckle," and "On a Honey Bee"—and, along with them, the poems that constitute their deistic, thus not quite Romantic, rationales, poems like "The Seasons Moralized," "On the Uniformity and Perfection of Nature," and "On the Religion of Nature.") The Freneau with whom I am concerned is he who would be at once satirist and celebrant—the poet who developed out of "The Rising Glory of America," from which I quoted at the outset. There is, for example, "A Political Litany," 1775:

> From a junto that labour with absolute power,
> Whose schemes disappointed have made them look sour,
> From the lords of the council, who fight against freedom,
> Who still follow on where delusion shall lead them.
>
> From the group at St. James's, who slight our petitions,
> And fools that are waiting for further submissions—
> From a nation whose manners are rough and severe,
> From scoundrels and rascals,—do keep us all clear.
>
>   * * *
>
> From the caitiff, lord *North*, who would bind us in chains,
> From a royal king *Log*, with his tooth-full of brains,
> Who dreams, and is certain (when taking a nap)
> He has conquered our lands, as they lay on his map.
>
> From a kingdom that bullies, and hectors, and swears,
> We send up to heaven our wishes and prayers

That we, disunited, may freemen be still,
And Britain go on—to be damned if she will.

This is the satirist, one example of him at work.

And this is an example of Freneau as celebrant, from his 1778 "American Independent; and Her Everlasting Deliverance from British Tyranny and Oppression." The poem begins:

'Tis done! and Britain for her madness sighs—
Take warning, tyrants and henceforth be wise,
If o'er mankind *man* gives you legal sway,
Take not the rights of human kind away.

Freneau goes on at great length to detail and interpret the history of the Revolution itself and his own part in it, and then begins his conclusion thus:

Let Turks and Russians glut their fields with blood,
Again let Britain dye the Atlantic flood,
Let all the east adore the sanguine wreathe
And gain new glories from the trade of death—
America! the works of peace be thine,
Thus shalt thou gain a triumph more divine—
To thee belongs a second golden reign,
Thine is the empire o'er a peaceful main;
Protect the rights of human kind below
Crush the proud tyrant who becomes their foe,
And future times shall own your struggles blest,
And future years enjoy perpetual rest.

In the end, I think, American Revolutionary poetry perforce becomes a poetry of celebration, with the satirical absorbed in and muffled by the celebratory. It is a proclamatory poetry, needfully so assertive that it cannot allow for the very doubts that its writers must surely have worked through to make their proclamations and assertions. Its depth is forced to the surface, in the process of which much— all that we know to have been integrally true of the Age of Paine—is lost. It culminates, once the Revolution is over, in a poem like David Humphreys's "Poem on the Industry of the United States of America," 1794, whose Revolution-empowered intention and aspirations are stated at the beginning:

Genius of Culture! thou, whose chaster taste
Can clothe with beauty ev'n the dreary waste;
Teach me to sing, what bright'ning charms unfold,
The bearded ears, that bend with more than gold,
How empire rises, and how morals spring,
From lowly labour, teach my lips to sing;
Exalt the numbers with thy gifts supreme,
Ennobler of the song, my guide and theme!

Humpreys had been a young man during the Revolution, as had his friend Joel Barlow, who in his epic of America, *The Columbiad* (1807), gave Columbus a vision of what was to come after the Revolution. Columbus sees

that other sapient band,
That torch of science flaming in their hand!
Thro nature's range their searching should aspire,
Or wake to life the canvass and the lyre.
Fixt in sublimest thought, behold them rise
World after world unfolding to their eyes,
Lead, light, allure them thro the total plan,
And give new guidance to the paths of man.

2

The great art, then, the great poetry, was yet to come, a product of the Revolution. It would follow that the art, the poetry, of the Revolution itself was only preparatory for something greater. The fact, of course, is that the poetry of the Revolution is not by any means major poetry. Freneau knew this, writing in his "To an Author," 1788:

An age employed in edging steel
Can no poetic raptures feel;
No solitude's attracting power,
No leisure of the noon day hour,
No shaded stream, no quiet grove
Can this fantastic century move . . .

John Adams, writing his wife from Paris, some time in 1780, reported on the beauties that he had seen and then commented:

It is not indeed the fine arts which our country requires; the useful, the mechanic arts are those which we have occasion for in a young country as yet simple and not far advanced in luxury, although perhaps much too far for her age and character. . . . I must study politics and war, that my sons may have liberty to study mathematics and philosophy. My sons ought to study mathematics and philosophy, geography, natural history and naval architecture, navigation, commerce, and agriculture, in order to give their children a right to study painting, poetry, music, architecture, statuary, and porcelain.[5]

Tom Paine put it more simply, remarking of himself in *The Age of Reason* (1794), "The natural bent of my mind was to science. I had some turn, and I believe some talent, for poetry; but this I rather repressed than encouraged, as leading too much into the field of imagination."[6]

Thus we should not too much regret, because not to be too much surprised at, the situation of American poetry in its Age of Paine. Further, we should recognize that this would seem to be a regular relationship between poetry and revolution, particularly when—so I have focused my remarks here—that poetry is to be *of* revolution. In 1924 Leon Trotsky outlined a possible version of the dialectics of the situation for us in our age:

> Culture feeds on the sap of economics, and a material surplus is necessary, so that culture may grow, develop and become subtle. Our bourgeoisie laid its hand on literature, and did this very quickly at the time when it was growing rich. The proletariat will be able to prepare the formation of a new, that is, a Socialist culture and literature, not by the laboratory method on the basis of our present-day poverty, want and illiteracy, but by large social, economic, and cultural means. Art needs comfort, even abundance. Furnaces have to be hotter, wheels have to move faster, looms have to turn more quickly, schools have to work better.[7]

Friedrich Engels, writing in 1885 to a correspondent who asked his advice about compiling an anthology of revolutionary poetry, was even more directly to the point: "In general, the poetry of past revolutions . . . rarely has a revolutionary effect for later times because it must also reproduce the mass prejudices of the period in order to affect the

5. *Familiar Letters of John Adams and His Wife Abigail* (New York: Hurd and Houghton, 1876), p. 381.
6. *Complete Writings*, ed. P. Foner (New York: Citadel Press, 1945), 1:496.
7. *Literature and Revolution* (1924; rpt. New York: Russell and Russell, 1957), pp. 9-11.

masses."[8] The point, I trust, can be well taken. If we can appreciate American Revolutionary poetry for what it was—a public poetry, a congeries of rhetorics, an uncritically celebratory poetry—we can rest satisfied and go on to a necessarily entailed question: What of Poetry, Revolution, and the Age of Paine *after* the fact? What follows, then, is a postscript, albeit a necessary postscript.

3

By the 1820s and 1830s, the visions of Freneau and Brackenridge, of Humphreys, and of Barlow seem to have been realized. It has been pointed out more than once that, although Rip Van Winkle awakens presumably in the 1790s, having slept through the Revolution, in effect he awakens in 1819, when Irving's story about him was first published. Westward-building, empire, urbanization, population growth, industrialization—all that marked American development and prosperity, all that we associate with what was to be the Age of Jackson and beyond—had set in. It is at this point—in retrospect, as it seems, inevitably—that the Revolution itself is taken as an enabling act, making possible a New America and the New Americans. Thus in his Fourth of July Oration in 1830, Edward Everett, speaking at Lowell, Massachusetts, could declare, "A prosperous manufacturing town like Lowell, regarded in itself, and as a specimen of other similar seats of American art and industry, may with propriety be considered as a peculiar triumph of our political independence. They are, if I may so express it, the complement of our political independence." Earlier in his oration, he had declared, "The astonishing growth [of the United States] has evidently not only been subsequent to the declaration of independence, but consequent upon its establishment, as effect upon cause."[9]

A literary analogue to Everett's (and so many others') statements is this, from the opening editorial pronouncement in the October 1837 *United States Magazine and Democratic Review*. Declaring that the "American Revolution was the greatest of experiments" and that the experiment was one of democratizing men, the editorialist went on to say:

8. *Marx and Engels on Literature and Art*, ed. L. Baxandall and S. Moriski (St. Louis: Telos Press, 1973), p. 128.
9. The address is anthologized in D. T. Miller, ed., *The Nature of Jacksonian America* (New York: Wiley, 1972), pp. 21-30.

The vital principle of an American national literature must be democracy. Our mind is enslaved to the past and present literature of England. . . . In the spirit of her literature we can never hope to rival England. . . . But we should not follow in her wake; a radiant path invites us forward in another direction. We have a principle, an informing soul, of our own, our democracy.[10]

It was also in 1837 that Emerson delivered "The American Scholar":

If there is any one period one would desire to be born in, is it not the age of Revolution; when the old and the new stand side by side and admit of being compared; when the energies of all men are searched by fear and hope; when the historic glories of the old can be compensated by the rich possibilities of the new era? This time, like all times, is a very good one, if we but know what to do with it.

By December 1839, he could write in his journal of a poetry fully democratized:

Treat Things Poetically.—Everything should be treated poetically,—law, politics, housekeeping, money. A judge and a banker must drive their craft poetically as well as a dancer or a scribe. . . . If you would write a code or logarithms, or a cookbook, you cannot spare the poetic impulse.

And by 1844, in "The Poet," he could fully envision his poet revolutionized:

We have yet had no genius in America, with tyrannous eye, which knew the value of our incomparable materials, and saw, in the barbarism and materialism of the times, another carnival of the same gods whose picture he so much admires in Homer; then in the Middle Age; then in Calvinism. . . . Our log-rolling, our stumps and their politics, our fisheries, our Negroes and Indians, our boasts and our repudiations, the wrath of rogues and the pusillanimity of honest men, the northern trade, the southern planting, the western clearing, Oregon and Texas, are yet unsung. Yet America is a poem in our eyes; its ample geography dazzles the imagination, and it will not wait long for meters.

Thus the democratic impulse in our literature, deriving from its revolu-

10. The editorial is anthologized in J. L. Blau, ed., *Social Theories of Jacksonian Democracy* (New York: Hoffmen Publishing Co., 1947), pp. 21-37.

tionary origins—the Revolution and what eventuated being conceived, as our historians have come recently to see it, as an Age of Paine.

Melville, writing to his friend Evert Duyckinck, 3 March 1849, put it most succinctly:

> —I would to God Shakspeare had lived later, & promenaded in Broadway. Not that I might have had the pleasure of leaving my card for him at the Astor, or made merry with him over a bowl of the fine Duyckinck punch; but that the muzzle which all men wore on their souls in the Elizebethan day, might not have intercepted Shakspers full articulations. For I hold it a verity that even Shakspeare, was not a frank man to the uttermost. And, indeed, who in this intolerant Universe is, or can be? But the Declaration of Independence makes a difference.[11]

The "difference"—that which would make possible Emerson's "tyrannous eye"—is an enabling factor, I am persuaded a crucial enabling factor, in American literature from the 1830s onward. But still, the possibility of the tyrannous eye and frankness notwithstanding, the American Revolution itself has not been much "available" to the American literary imagination for full and open (or open-ended) treatment. I suspect that it is a matter of the unavailability of a sense of the Revolutionary period as an Age of Paine. For surely, what a writer of the highest sensibility needs is a view of a segment of history that absolutely comports with his tyrannous and frank sense of the fullness and depth of human nature working its way, for good and for bad, through its history.

Even in that period of our literature culminating in the American Renaissance, that Revolution-inspired period as Emerson called it, most of the writing that takes an aspect of the Revolution for its subject is celebratory, its subject conceived in terms that define its public, not its private, dimensions. There are Cooper's *The Spy* (1821), Simms's *The Partisan* (1835) and the five other Revolutionary historical romances that followed it, and Kennedy's *Horse-Shoe Robinson* (1835)—to recall the major titles. As for poetry itself, there is Emerson's ennobling but not penetrating "Concord Hymn" (1837), Longfellow's ballad-like "Paul Revere's Ride" (1860), and a series of odes on Revolutionary subjects by Lowell, beginning in 1849 and ending in 1876 and increasing in stiffness and pomposity. The purview of these poems—and there are others,

11. *Letters*, ed. M. Davis and W. Gilman (New Haven: Yale University Press, 1960), pp. 79-80.

even lesser, like them—suggests the purview of the poetry deriving immediately from the Revolution itself, except of course for the lack of committed satire. Emerson, Longfellow, and Lowell in their poems take upon themselves the responsibility for public, communal celebration. And it is not appropriate in such celebration to go deep. What is called for—and given—is affirmation, yea saying. Each of these poets—indeed, each of the romancers I have instanced—was on other occasions, though varyingly and unsurely, capable of going deep, of saying Yes only after he had chanced saying No. But not as regards the American Revolution.

I know of only three instances in the writing of the American Renaissance where the writer is able to cut through received tradition and memory, so to catch a glimpse of the Revolutionary and post-Revolutionary period as an Age of Paine. Two of these, since they are fiction (though as romances, they are on the edge of being poetry), I can note only in passing.

There is Hawthorne's great tale, "My Kinsman, Major Molineux" (1832), in which in immediately pre-Revolutionary times a young man, Robin Molineux, comes to the city from the country, seeking his kinsman and his fortune. He is a Molineux, since his sought-for kinsman is his paternal uncle. After a series of nightmarish encounters, he does find his kinsman, but as the loyalist tarred-and-feathered victim of a revolutionary mob. (Think of Trumball's *M'Fingal*.) He becomes part of that mob, and so must learn something, in the deepest personal terms, of revolution, political and otherwise. The tormentor and the tormented—thus the rebel and he against whom he rebels—somehow are one. Moreover, in one of Hawthorne's major ironies, the name given Robin and his kinsman is in the fact that of one of the principal, most violent of revolutionary tormentors and persecutors of loyalists. In the tale, revolution—however properly it ends—is conceived as implicating the self and the other, the rebel and him against whom he rebels, in a process at once destructive and constructive. Its pain is not, cannot, be blinked. Hawthorne intends us to be witnesses of our own beginnings and, in the witnessing, to be willing to acknowledge the price paid for what we have achieved. An Age of Paine indeed.[12]

12. For details, see my "Hawthorne and the Sense of the Past; or, The Immortality of Major Molineux," *Historicism Once More* (Princeton: Princeton University Press, 1969), pp. 137-45.

There is Melville's *Israel Potter* (1855), dedicated "To His Highness, The Bunker Hill Monument," which began its appearance in *Putnam's Monthly Magazine*, July 1854, as "A Fourth of July Story." It is once a heroic and an anti-heroic tale. Israel is a wanderer, whose various adventures always conclude with his being down-and-out. Long gone from his home in Vermont, he fights at Bunker Hill, is captured by the British, taken to England, befriended by rebel agents, becomes a secret courier between England and France, meets Franklin and John Paul Jones, fights alongside Jones, in confusion gets to England again, sees Ethan Allen as captive, settles in disguise in London, lives out his life in poverty until at the end of his "Fifty Years of Exile" he returns to the United States, seeking a pension, which of course is denied—as he, so strong a believer in the Revolutionary cause, is in fact denied his American identity most of his life. The portraits of Franklin, Jones, and Allen are at once hugely comic and gross, as is Israel's life. Warfare is described graphically and unpityingly. The Revolution and its aftermath as regards Israel are interpreted in Melville's conclusion at the end of the sequence of chapters in which he describes the fight between the *Serapis* and the *Bon Homme Richard*, in which Israel participated:

> The loss of life in the two ships was about equal; one-half of the total number of those engaged being killed or wounded.
>
> In view of this battle one may ask—What separates the enlightened man from the savage? Is civilization a thing distinct, or is it an advanced stage of barbarism?

Israel, as the tale moves toward its end, is the anti-hero as scapegoat. "Requiescat in Pace" the last chapter is called. And old Israel, his exile ended, is shown, on the Fourth of July, looking at Bunker Hill:

> Upon those heights, fifty years before, his now feeble hands had wielded both ends of the musket. There too he had received that slit upon the chest, which afterwards, in the affair with the Serapis, being traversed with a cutlass wound, made him now the bescarred bearer of a cross.

Scarred with the cross of the Revolution. Black comedy in the Age of Paine.

The third instance is in verse, what became in its final version the thirty-fifth and the thirty-sixth sections of Whitman's "Song of

Myself." The sections are part of the fourth phase of the poem, that in which, as I have written,[13] we are to know the poet (as person) fully at home in his newly defined world, fully sure of himself and of what he can declare: "I am an acme of things accomplish'd, and I am encloser of things to be." Sections thirty-five and thirty-six deal with the battle between the *Bon Homme Richard* and the *Serapis*, about which Whitman learned from his maternal grandmother, whose father had served under John Paul Jones, and from a recently published account of the battle by Jones himself. I follow here the version of "Song of Myself" given in the 1855 *Leaves of Grass*, which has an involved directness considerably attenuated in later versions.

Following his account of the Battle of the Alamo, which immediately precedes these sections, Whitman begins:

> Did you read in the seabooks of the oldfashioned frigate-fight?
> Did you learn who won by the light of the moon and stars?
>
> Our foe was no skulk in his ship, I tell you,
> His was the English pluck, and there is no tougher or truer,
>   and never was, and never will be;
> Along the lowered eve he came, horribly raking us.
>
> We closed with him. . . . the yards tangled. . . . the
>   cannon touched,
> My captain lashed fast with his own hands.

A bloody description, almost surrealistic, follows. Then:

> Toward twelve at night, there in the beams of the moon they
>   surrendered to us.
> Stretched and still lay the midnight,
> Two great hulls motionless on the breast of the darkness,
> Our vessel riddled and slowly sinking. . . . preparations to
> pass to the one we had conquered,
> The captain on a quarter deck coldly giving his orders
>   through a countenance white as sheet,
> Near by the corpse of the child that served in the cabin,
> The dead face of an old salt with long white hair and
>   carefully curled whiskers,
> The flames spite of all that could be done flickering aloft
>   and below,

13. Cf. my *Continuity of American Poetry* (Princeton: Princeton University Press, 1961), p. 74.

> The husky voices of the two or three officers yet fit for
>   duty,
> Formless stacks of bodies and bodies by themselves. . . .
>   dabs of flesh upon the masts and spars,
> The cut of cordage and the dangle of rigging. . . .the slight
>   shock of the soothe of the waves,
> Black and impassive guns, and litter of powder-parcels, and
>   the strong scent,
> Delicate sniff of the seabreeze. . . .smells of sedgy grass
>   and fields by the shore. . . .death-messages given in
>   charge to survivors,
> The hiss of the surgeon's knife and the gnawing teeth of his
>   saw,
> The wheeze, the cluck, the swash of falling blood. . . .the
>   short wild scream, the long tapering groan,
> These so. . . .these irretrievable.

The details are as hard-hitting and as frank as those in Hawthorne's description of the tarred-and-feathered Major Molineux and Melville's of the battles in which Israel Potter fought. Whitman's way of comprehending such details, comprehending them in all their painfulness, is consonant with, in this phase of "Song of Myself," his way of comprehending the world he is discovering—as "acme of things accomplish'd," so that, with him, we are to accept our past (as also our present and our future) wholly for what it has been, therefore is. He goes on immediately in the 1855 version after the passage I have quoted:

> O Christ; My fit is mastering me!
> What the rebel said gaily adjusting his throat to the rope-
>   noose,
> What the savage at the stump, his eye-sockets empty, his
>   mouth spirting whoops and defiance,
> What still the traveler come to the vault at Mount Vernon,
> What sobers the Brooklyn boy as he looks down the shores of
>   the Wallabout and remembers the prison ships,
> What burnt the gums of the redcoat at Saratoga when he
>   surrendered his brigades,
> These become mine and me very one, and they are but little,
>
> I become as much more as I like.
> I become any presence or truth of humanity here,
> And see myself in prison shaped like another man,
> And feel the dull unintermitted pain.

There follow, as "Song of Myself" works out its special dialectic, accounts of other sorts of pain, and also of other sorts of glory. The poet would lead us to comprehend, so to live with, so to accept the responsibility that makes for the promise of, ourselves in our history—in this instance, our Age of Paine. Not in dreams, but in our history, so comprehended, begin our responsibilities—and our freedom.

4

I know of no other nineteenth-century poetic text that deals so tellingly with our Revolution as does Whitman's. Indeed, as my reader will have gathered, I know very few texts—poetic or otherwise—that do so. We can, because we must, accept the quality of poetry produced directly out of the Revolutionary situation for what it was—so involved, so "ideological," so tendentious, so celebratory as to make it consist of so many public pronouncements, self-assured, therefore assuring us. So too with Emerson, Longfellow, and Lowell on Revolutionary themes. And of course what we ask of poetry—and of literature generally—is not that it assure us but that it enlighten us, that it establish a vital tie between our most deeply possible selves and the history of the world in which those selves have been shaped.

For whatever reason, the Revolution as theme, as topos, has not been available to the American literary imagination in a way that would lead to poems and fictions that might enlighten us. There are interesting enough twentieth-century novels on the theme—those by Gore Vidal, Kenneth Roberts, Walter D. Edmunds, Howard Fast, for example. But, for all their sophistication in sociocultural detail, these novels lack (to use Henry James's phrase about Hawthorne) the "deeper psychology" we must require of major fiction. There are the sections devoted to John Adams in Ezra Pound's *Cantos*. But these are mainly documentary and, as poetry, are sustained—if in fact they are—only by their being embedded in a context so global as to lack the power of historicity. In my reading I have encountered three recent poems on Revolutionary themes—Robert Bly's "Poem Against the British," Frank O'Hara's "On Seeing Larry Rivers' *Washington Crossing the Delaware* at the Museum of Modern Art," and Diane Wakowski's *George Washington Poems* sequence. Each figures a relationship between the poet in our time and Washington as a kind of Revolutionary father figure. In all, however, the Revolution is discovered, or invented, as occasion, not felt cause.

During the period 1775-1825, the Revolution is so much, so directly, the cause of its poetry that, as I have said, the poems produced are, understandably enough, overdetermined, meant so much to move and urge that they do not allow for that meditation in tranquillity and working-through—what Whitman called vivification—that are necessary conditions of full poetic achievement. We realize now, as I pointed out at the beginning, that the Revolution itself, precisely because it was a revolution, a genuine revolution, was overdetermined. Meditation and working-through, vivification, were irrelevant because, in the situation, virtually impossible. In point of fact, the situation itself was felt to be self-vivifying. Thus, through the work of our recent historians, our sense of the Age of Paine. But from 1825 or so onward, that overdetermination came to exist as a memory; and so cause for the most part became occasion, the tone of the occasion being set by recollection and pathos. For the writer of great power, however, for poems and stories of great power, an occasion, even one out of the past, must be felt strongly enough to become a cause—a cause, as I have said, meditated in tranquillity and worked through—vivified. This is how the high literary imagination works when it deals with its own history. Thus Hawthorne, Melville, and above all Whitman. Perhaps our historians' new understanding of the American Revolution will become available to the literary imagination, so that occasion can indeed become cause, and our poets, like Whitman, will rise to that special occasion which was and is the Revolution, discover a cause, vivify it, and so be able to say:

> I become any presence or truth of humanity here. . . .

1976/1986

4

A SENSE OF THE PRESENT:
HAWTHORNE AND
THE HOUSE OF THE SEVEN GABLES

On 15 March 1851, Nathaniel Hawthorne, then in his forty-seventh year, wrote his closest friend, Horatio Bridge:

> The House of the Seven Gables, in my opinion is better than The Scarlet Letter; but I should not wonder if I had refined upon the principal character a little too much for popular appreciation; nor if the romance of the book should be found somewhat at odds with the humble and familiar scenery in which I invest it. But I feel that portions of it are as good as anything I can hope to write, and the publisher speaks encouragingly of its success.
>
> How slowly I have made my way in life! How much is still to be done! How little worth (outwardly, I mean) is all that I have achieved! The "buble reputation" is as much a bubble in literature as in war; and I should not be one whit the happier if mine were world-wide and time-long than I was when nobody but yourself had faith in me. The only sensible ends of literature are, first, the pleasurable toil in writing; secondly, the gratification of one's family and friends, and, lastly the solid cash.[1]

Hawthorne as correspondent was always most honest and open when he was writing to Bridge. They were of course college classmates; Bridge, without informing Hawthorne, had arranged for the publication of his first collection, *Twice-Told Tales*, in 1837; Hawthorne had advised on and edited for publication—and, in editing added to—Bridge's *Journal of an African Cruiser* in 1845 and indeed was trying to help Bridge with a new edition of that book in 1851 when he wrote the letter from which I have quoted. And it was Bridge who became Hawthorne's principal contact with official Washington immediately

1. I quote Hawthorne here, as always, from the Centenary Edition of his *Works*.

before and during the period when Hawthorne served as American con-
sul in Liverpool, having been appointed by their college friend President
Franklin Pierce, in part as recompense for having written Pierce's campaign biography, concerning which Bridge was one of Hawthorne's
principal informants. And Hawthorne in 1852 dedicated his last collection, *The Snow-Image*, to Bridge. In that dedication, publicly acknowledging Bridge's crucial role in his development as a "fiction-monger,"
Hawthorne figured his history as a writer this way:

> But, was there ever such a weary delay in obtaining the slightest
> recognition from the public, as in my case? I sat down by the wayside of
> life, like a man under enchantment, and a shrubbery sprung up around
> me, and the bushes grew to be saplings, and the saplings became trees,
> until no exit appeared possible, through the entangling depths of my
> obscurity. And there, perhaps, I should be sitting at this moment, with
> the moss on the imprisoning tree-trunks, and the yellow leaves of more
> than a score of autumns piled above me, if it had not been for you.

I make this much of Hawthorne's relation to Bridge not because I
wish to sketch a biography but because I want to establish the authenticity, as regards what we might call Hawthorne's discontents, of the 15
March 1851 letter. What Hawthorne is saying—and he says it elsewhere,
to other, for him, lesser correspondents—is that at long last he has
written the sort of book that he has wanted to, that *The House of the
Seven Gables* is genuinely his. And my principal concern is *The House of
the Seven Gables*. I hope that, by putting that romance firmly in the
context of Hawthorne's career, I can read it in such a way as to make it
genuinely ours, as it has, I think, become genuinely mine.

With the publication in March 1850 of *The Scarlet Letter*, Hawthorne
was at long last free from the necessity of writing short pieces, for
which he was often badly paid, for gift books and magazines. He was
free of the burden of spending a good deal of time catering to a public
whose tastes, so his correspondence shows, he found suspect. Or, I
should say, he was almost free. For even as, after the publication of *The
Scarlet Letter*, he moved toward and into the writing of *The House of the
Seven Gables* and after that *The Blithedale Romance* and his two books for
children (the latter three of which he also felt to be genuinely his)—even
as he was free to do such writing, he was under pressure to see all his
earlier work put back into print. Indeed, he had played it cautiously

with *The Scarlet Letter*, working up the long Custom House preface so as to guide his reader relatively comfortably into his (as he described it to Bridge in a letter of 4 February 1850) "h—ll-fired story." Reporting that, as he had predicted, *The Scarlet Letter* was indeed a publishing success, Hawthorne's publisher (who soon became a friend) James T. Fields began in March 1850 to urge Hawthorne to let his firm, Ticknor and Fields, put all of Hawthorne's earlier collections back into print and also to keep the firm supplied with new material. Thus in March 1851 came a new edition of *Twice-Told Tales* for which Hawthorne supplied a new preface; Fields was in such a hurry to get the book back into print that he persuaded Hawthorne that there was no time to modify or revise the collection or to allow its author to read proof. In November 1851 came a new edition of *True Stories from History and Biography*, a collection of four hackwork juveniles that Hawthorne had put together without much enthusiasm, except to make some money, in the early 1840s. In December of that year—on a suggestion from Fields—came a new collection of old pieces—in many cases the pieces had to be almost literally scraped from the bottom of the barrel—to which Hawthorne gave the name *The Snow-Image* and about which he commented ruefully in his dedicatory preface to Bridge:

> Some of these sketches were among the earliest that I wrote, and, after lying for years in manuscript, they at last skulked into the Annuals or Magazines, and have hidden themselves there ever since. Others were the productions of a later period; others, again, were written recently. The comparison of these various trifles—the indices of intellectual condition at far separated epochs—affects me with a singular complexity of regrets.

The republication, with additions once more scraped from the bottom of the barrel, of *Mosses from an Old Manse* did not come until October 1854, but only because Fields, who had written Hawthorne about the matter as early as March 1851, could not secure rights to the plates from the original publisher until the later date. In January 1851 Fields even tried to get Hawthorne to let him republish *Fanshawe*, the deliberately and crudely sales-oriented piece that had appeared anonymously in 1828 and that Hawthorne had long since tried to suppress. Fields's sense of his own role is put succinctly in a letter of 12 March 1851 chock-full of publishing suggestions: "To 'keep the pot a boiling' has always been the endeavor of all true Yankees from the days of the Colonies down to the present era. "

Because he needed the money, Hawthorne let himself be guided by Fields. He knew perfectly well the difference between his achieved, authentic tales and sketches and those that were inauthentic, therefore unachieved. Indeed, he had designed *Twice-Told Tale* and *Mosses* to contain something for everybody, a mixture of seriously conceived tales and sketches and those that would appeal to a readership looking merely for sentimental entertainment. And he designed *The Snow Image* the same way. That was the honestly commercial side of his mind. I think that his ambiguity about the value of these earlier productions is expressed in the introductions to the volumes—those to the first and third named, recall, written explicitly in a reprint situation. In any case, it is in this context of keeping the pot boiling—often with potboiler material— that he conceived of *The House of the Seven Gables*, that he designed and executed a romance that would at long last let him be altogether true to his own sense of his vocation as writer. He would somehow have to transcend the discontents that disturbed him as he, reprint after reprint, reviewed his whole career, his whole past. Doing so, he would discover himself in the present. Awaiting Bridge's opinion of *The House of the Seven Gables*, he wrote his friend 22 July 1851:

> I rather think I have reached that stage where I do not care very essentially one way or the other, for anybody's opinion on any one production. On this last Romance, for instance, I have heard and seen such diversity of judgment, that I should be altogether bewildered if I attempted to strike a balance;—so I take nobody's estimate, unless it happens to agree with my own. I think it a work more characteristic of my mind, and more proper and natural for me to write, than the Scarlet Letter—But, for that very reason, less likely to interest the public. Nevertheless it appears to have sold better than the former, and, I think, is more sure of retaining the ground it acquires.

The question to which here I address myself centers on "the ground" that *The House of the Seven Gables* acquires and how it may be retained.

In his preface, Hawthorne, in a definition that of course has proved fateful for the evolution of American fiction and our understanding of it, calls his work a Romance. He says of the Romance, as opposed to the Novel, that, "as a work of art, it must rigidly subject itself to laws, and while it sins unpardonably, so far as it may swerve aside from the truths of the human heart—has fairly a right to present that truth under circumstances, to a great extent, of the writer's own choosing or creation." A little further on, he writes: "The point of view in which this tale comes under the Romantic definition lies in the attempt to connect a bygone time with the very present time that is flitting away from us." Then: "the author has provided himself with a moral,—the truth, namely, that the wrong-doing of one generation lives into the successive ones, and, divesting itself of every temporary advantage, becomes a pure and uncontrollable mischief." After expanding this statement somewhat, Hawthorne pulls back and says that if his Romance is to teach, to have "any effective operation, it is usually through a far more subtle process than the ostensible one." Only thus may the "high truth" of art be achieved; but, he adds, in effect, if that truth is to be authentic, it must somehow not be developed, or argued, or unfolded, but manifested from the beginning to the end. It must, in short, be both the cause of the Romance and its effect.

The House of the Seven Gables, then, is to be a Romance in which history—the continuity of communal guilt in history—is manifested in such a way that the past is connected dynamically, in moral actuality, to the present. The present we must note, the preface bids us note, is not only the present of the characters in the Romance—Hepzibah and Clifford Pyncheon, Judge Jaffrey Pyncheon, Phoebe, Holgrave, and the others who inhabit their world. The present is not only theirs, but it is Hawthorne's. Moreover, it is that of Hawthorne's readers—including, if the "operation" is truly "effective," those meditating on the Romance as they read these words.

Hawthorne, I am saying, is proposing that *The House of the Seven Gables* be a Romance of the present by virtue of being a Romance of the past and vice versa. He is proposing that it be an altogether perfected historical work—perfected in the etymological sense of that word, carried through all the way into the immediate present; that through its art we discover our history and seal it to our present, so as to define ourselves in the present. He had tried to do this earlier in *The Scarlet Letter*, but in a curiously different way. For there it is the Custom House preface that functions to seal past to present, as Hawthorne, however playfully, reminds himself and us of his ancestor's sins and tells us that it is in fact his ancestors who have bid him write this book, thus sealing past to present. In *The House of the Seven Gables* the process, the "effective operation," works, as Hawthorne says in the preface, more subtly. For "effective operation" is in Hawthorne's vocabulary a somewhat technical term, referring to the psychological process, as we might call it, that is set off and guided by works of the creative imagination. "Effective operation" is postulated on the faith that there is a "truth of the human heart," which can be evoked, referred to, strengthened; whose scope can be enlarged. Specifically, in *The House of the Seven Gables* the scope must be sufficiently enlarged to take into account—so to accommodate—the facts, the factuality, of history. Otherwise that heart will not be quite human enough, because not quite true enough—not true enough to its own capacity to be true.

I think that Hawthorne went to such great pains to prepare us to see this because, under the pressure of willy-nilly reviewing much of his earlier work, he recognized that his newest Romance was not quite of a piece with *The Scarlet Letter*, much less with the tales and sketches for which he had so far been best known. Also, he wanted to signal the fact that he was beginning to do something new, that at long last he had begun to realize his authentic vocation; or rather, that he was beginning to work out a new, more broadly and inclusively conceived variation on his central theme. In what follows I want (1) to speak about that central theme and its variations; (2) to speak of the anticipation of what I shall call *The House of the Seven Gables* variation on that theme in Hawthorne's earlier—indeed, earliest—work; and (3) to elucidate and judge its "effective operation" in *The House of the Seven Gables*.

1. *Hawthorne's central theme* is of course that of his great nineteenth-century peers—the discovery of self: ironically, the discovery of self in a culture whose worshipful devotion to the idea of self had increasingly become nominal. The idea of self is everywhere celebrated in mid-nineteenth-century writing—not only the idea of self, but also the idea of community as it might be derived from the idea of self. Indeed, the definition of community was as an amalgamation of selves, authentic selves. How move from selfhood, authentic selfhood, to community? This was the overriding question that Hawthorne and his peers asked themselves. And their answers vary—from, say, Melville's vision of men as ineluctably "isolatoes" (in his word from *Moby-Dick*) to Whitman's vision of a direct, willed transvaluation of selfhood into community. However great the range of answers—which is, in effect, the range

of mid-nineteenth-century American writing—the necessary condition of the answers is by all taken to be identical: the discovery, or rediscovery, of self. I once more think a couple of sentences from Emerson's essay "Experience" put it best, as I think that that essay is *the* place to begin the study of American literature. The statement goes like this: "It is too late to be helped, the discovery we have made that we exist. That discovery is called the Fall of Man."

The discovery of the existence of self—of its inextricably bound components of good and evil, innocence and guilt, love and death. The Hawthorne of *The Scarlet Letter* and the tales and sketches—under which, for the sake of my argument, may be subsumed the pre-*Seven Gables* Hawthorne—that Hawthorne works a variation on the central theme as he shows individuals coming to know their innermost selves as they hurt and are hurt. They come, in effect, to know who and what they really are; they must draw apart from society—or they do things that force society to drive them out of its ambiance: emphasis is not on the origin of the self they discover, but on its nature and immediate quality. Thus their fall into existence. The plot-making question must always be: What will be the immediate outcome of a discovery of self whose innocence and guilt are inextricably one? Some, Young Goodman Brown and Wakefield, for example, are completely destroyed—the one with his enjoying power atrophied, the other with his ability to go home lost. Some few survive; Hester in *The Scarlet Letter* is the great example. Hester's acknowledged guilt is humblingly educative; it takes its "effective operation" as she becomes—except for those moments when her dark passion reminds us of her essential nature—virtually an angel on earth. The emphasis in the stories that work this variation is on the present—that is, the past as it *was* the present. But of course we always wonder how it will be in the future—what will happen to Young Goodman Brown and Wakefield? And we know that Little Pearl, in *The Scarlet Letter*, is in the end, through Hester's and Dimmesdale's open acknowledgment of her, released to become a woman, to have a future. What will happen to her? This Hawthorne will not tell us that. The Hawthorne of *The House of the Seven Gables* is different.

I suggest that it is just this concern for the future that led Hawthorne to that variation on the major theme which he goes to such pains to outline in the preface to *The House of the Seven Gables*. If in the first the emphasis is on the need to withdraw in the present, so to return and make the future (Little Pearl's future) possible, then the emphasis in the second is on the need to return to the present, to make the future actual. The future in *The House of the Seven Gables* is of course Phoebe's and Holgrave's. Each has, in his and her own way, been cut off from society; each has already begun to discover authentic selfhood. But it is a selfhood that will not be adequate unless it be matured in society. And maturing, growth, is impossible unless it be a growth from the past, into the present, toward the future. For when the nineteenth-century American (I mean the nineteenth-century American as Hawthorne understood him), having discovered his selfhood, came to return to the world, he found that one of its vital constituents was its past, *his* past—its history, *his* history. Acknowledgment that he was caught in its history, that its history was his—this constituted the plot-making "effective operation" of stories of the sort that Hawthorne told. The logic, however, was not only Hawthorne's. It was that of his culture—one of the principal components of his civilization's discontents. It might well remain so. Indeed, if his Romance has now a wholly "effective operation," it must in significant part remain so for us.

2. I turn now to my second topic, *Hawthorne's earlier anticipation of the Seven Gables theme*: his concern—his imminent concern—with the past as it might, when fully comprehended, be acknowledged in the present; with the past as it might be sealed to the present, so to make the future not only possible but actual.

As early as 1829, Hawthorne was hoping to publish a series of inter-related stories to be called *Provincial Tales*. Five of these stories survive; and of the five, four anticipate, only that, what I have called the *Seven Gables* version of Hawthorne's central theme. They are "My Kinsman, Major Molineux," "Roger Malvin's Burial," "The Gentle Boy," and "Alice Doane's Appeal." That is, their "effective operation" is the product of a discovery that to come into the present world, the present community, is to come into its history and to realize once and for all that that history is one's own: for good and for bad, one's own. That discovery turns out to be a necessary condition for moving from the present into the future.

The most important of these stories is "My Kinsman, Major Molineux." We have only fairly recently come to see in it one of

Hawthorne's major achievements. And here I must repeat, in summary version, what I have already written about it.[2]

It begins with a curiously pompous paragraph, in which Hawthorne, parodying received notions of the idea of progress, rationalizes *ex post facto* what he is about to describe, and so in effect would appear to be constructing an apologia for all revolutionary violence as the unfortunate but necessary result of a "train of circumstances that had caused much temporary inflammation of the popular mind." Hawthorne's sophisticated readers would have recognized in this paragraph the style and rhetoric of the American historian of the first quarter of the nineteenth century, whether he be liberal or conservative. For such a historian the Revolutionary War was once and for all over and its violence now had to be understood in such a way as to be put out of mind; it had to be understood as a necessary effect of that law of progress which the Revolution had so clearly and powerfully realized. But Hawthorne will not let it be so. His position, which he would have be his readers' position, in the rest of the story is one he put succinctly a quarter of a century later in his campaign biography of his college-mate Franklin Pierce: "There is no instance, in all history, of the human will and intellect having perfected any moral reform by methods which it adapted to that end; but the progress of the world, at every step, leaves some evil or wrong on the path behind it, which the wisest of mankind, of their own set purpose, could never have found a way to rectify." "My Kinsman, Major Molineux" is thus an account of an episode in "the progress of the world," so understood.

The episode is one in the life of young Robin Molineux (we are never *told* that his family name is Molineux; but since he seeks his father's brother, we can assume it—so to learn that we *have* to assume it). In Revolutionary times he comes to Boston at night, seeking his well-to-do kinsman and his fortune. He is all self-assurance; for his kinsman is wealthy and important; everyone will know him. In a series of bewildering, nightmarish adventures, he fails to find his kinsman. No one will tell him anything. So he sits down in front of a church—it is now the middle of the night—and watches and waits. It turns out that

2. See my "Hawthorne and the Sense of the Past; or, The Immortality of Major Molineux," *Historicism Once More: Problems and Occasions for the American Scholar* (Princeton: Princeton University Press, 1969), pp. 137-74.

he watches and waits for his history. For a mad procession comes along in the midst of which, dragged in a cart, is Robin's kinsman—a Tory, a Loyalist, now being tormented, tarred and feathered by his fellows, who want only their freedom. Robin is at first frightened, then drawn hypnotically into the mob. Its members roar with laughter at their victim. And, compulsively, Robin roars with laughter too—makes no attempt to go to the help of his kinsman, his uncle, his father's brother. But each recognizes the other. Further, without having meant to, Robin seems—only seems—to recognize himself. And at the end we are left wondering, as *he* is, whether he will stay in the city and make his fortune or return to the country. The idea of progress, as Robin lives through one of its revolutionary, therefore violent, moments, is a *rite de passage.*

The mob that Robin joins is, as Hawthorne's pompous opening paragraph indicates, only one of many such during the Revolutionary (or rather, pre-Revolutionary) period. What Hawthorne does is to look at the mob, and at the revolutionary necessity that it embodies, not in terms of what is brought about but in terms of the bringing about, the act, the experience, in itself. There is no indication that Hawthorne would reject what has been brought about; a *fait accompli* is a *fait accompli.* But he would have his protagonist Robin pay for it—pay by discovering that if he is to the heir of his history, then he must take all his heritage and live with it. If he can bear to, that is. But further, Hawthorne would make his American readers understand their full heritage. He would do so by destroying and then replacing the rationalizations of the opening paragraph of the story—a parody, I repeat, of the style and rhetoric, and of the content, of the sort of history books that Americans read and believed in—by replacing those rationalizations with a vital sense of what is antecedent to them and what must take their place. The irony in this instance is all the more powerful when we realize, as some of Hawthorne's contemporaries must have, that the story is shot through with quite exact historical references and allusions—the most important of which is contained, in a brilliantly ironic reversal, in the fact that Hawthorne used the name *Molineux* precisely because it was in actuality the name of a notorious leader of Revolutionary mobs—a tormentor, not one of the tormented. So that we must conclude that he started with Robin Molineux as mobster and then invented his kinsman, he who was tormented, since he wanted to tell us that in destroying men to make progress we inevitably destroy part of ourselves and cannot have any hope of being whole again unless we learn to live with the knowledge and somehow expiate it. How expiate it? And what has the expiation to do with moving from this present into the future? That I think is central to the matter of *The House of the Seven Gables*.

3. And so I come to my third topic, *The House of the Seven Gables* itself and Hawthorne's sense of it, as he viewed the old and the new in his work, as being—in his words to Bridge—"a work more characteristic of my mind, and more proper and natural for me to write, than The Scarlet Letter." I return to that point in *The House of the Seven Gables* where I paused in my discussion of it, at the end of the preface, with its blatant declaration of the moral of the Romance.

There are, I remind its readers, equally blatant remarks throughout the Romance. Once Hawthorne speaks, almost in terms of nineteenth-century evolutionary theory, of drawing "a mighty lesson from the little-regarded truth, that the act of the passing generation is the germ which may and must produce good or evil fruit in a far-distant time." He makes the House itself and its surroundings project just this "truth"—in a pattern of symbol and metaphor that has been much remarked by interpreters of the Romance. In statement and in image, the idea occurs again and again. In the end, one tends to drop the charge of blatantness or over-explicitness, because one comes to see that Hawthorne's point of view is that of the historian: the historian, as it were, *in extremis*, the historian engagé; the historian who will not stop with extracting a moral from the data of history but will make those data part of the moral sensibility of his readers, just as they are part of the moral sensibility of his characters. It is of the essence that the past be sealed to the present. Thus Hawthorne's hopes for the "effective operation" of his Romance. After he has traced the history of the Pyncheons and the Maules in the first chapter, he can justifiably, because necessarily, conclude of the Pyncheon's legal tenure in the Seven Gables property that:

> of their legal tenure, there could be no question; but old Matthew Maules, it is to be feared, trode downward from his own age to a far later one, planting a heavy footstep, all the way, on the conscience of a Pyncheon. If so, we are left to dispose of the awful query, whether each

inheritor of the property—conscious of wrong, and failing to rectify it—did not commit anew the great guilt of his ancestor, and incur all its original responsibilities. And supposing such to be the case, would it not be a truer mode of expression to say, of the Pyncheon family, that they inherited a great misfortune, than the reverse?

This is terrible enough, I think. But, if only we think through the dialectic of the Romance as it is to develop from this thesis, there is something more terrible: In fact, the later Pyncheons could never fully expiate the earlier, the original, sin. At most, they could make some amends to others. As for themselves, they could make amends only by living with themselves and the vital memory of what they had become. Living with that memory, they might have disciplined themselves into that sort of life wherein they might be able continually to fight the temptation to revert to type, and so continually to live in the world, perhaps love in the world.

This is, I think, the essence of the "moral" of *The House of the Seven Gables*, as it is to work its "effective operation"—the paradox of man's history is that the more he acknowledges his complicity in its inevitable sinfulness, the more he is at once tempted to revert to type and the more he knows he must resist the temptation. Reverting to type (as does Judge Pyncheon), he lives in the present by a kind of repetition compulsion derived from the past. Not reverting to type, but knowing how and what it would be to do so, he can look toward the future, walk into the future, never quite pulling out his roots in the past, indeed securing those roots.

For in the Romance, the world of Hepzibah and Clifford Pyncheon is dead. This is how they sense what it is to live in the present. Something out of their past has contaminated their world; yet something in their immediate present has actually killed it. Thus in the second chapter, Hawthorne comments on Hepzibah's pitiful attempts to open her little shop:

> In this Republican county, amid the fluctuating waves of our social life, somebody is always at the drowning-point. The tragedy is enacted with as continued a repetition as that of a popular drama on a holiday; and, nevertheless, is felt as deeply, perhaps, as when an hereditary noble sinks below his order. More deeply; since, with us, rank is the grosser substance of wealth and a splendid establishment, and has no spiritual existence after the death of these, but dies hopelessly along with them.

To say this is to discover an element of tragedy and suffering necessarily inherent in social progress. Moreover, since the original corruption is the Pyncheons', social progress would seem to be understood as the agent whereby that which is corrupt and contaminated is done away with. The tragedy is that of the person of good (if weak) will in whom that corruption and contamination are currently manifest. It would thus be exclusively Hepzibah's and Clifford's tragedy.

But, to extrapolate the words of the preface, all persons inherit the wrongdoing of the past, so that, somehow, all persons must be involved in this tragedy—and, if they can acknowledge their involvement, must be shown equally to share in whatever triumph may follow. Such, at any rate, seems to me to have been Hawthorne's intention in composing *The House of the Seven Gables* as he did. For the Romance, considered in terms of its announced and reiterated intention, does not center on Hepzibah and Clifford Pyncheon but on Phoebe (who is only partly a Pyncheon) and on Holgrave (who is a Maule). They must be made to bear the burden of history as much as Hepzibah and Clifford; only they must be made, unlike Hepzibah and Clifford, to come through to some sense of triumph—to live in the present so as to actualize the future. The perfection of *The House of the Seven Gables*, Hawthorne's carrying it through to the end, entails the perfection of all who figure in it, each to the proper degree.

Surely, the portraits of Hepzibah and Clifford are superb. There is the old maid soured against her will, holding firmly to her little pride, trying to make her brother happy, so held by her rotten roots in the past that she can neither break free from them nor gain from them such nurture as will make her a whole person. There is Clifford—shattered by his history. He is childishly sensuous, now blowing soap bubbles into the street, now falling into the deep sleep of a child, but a child no longer capable of a genuine sense of innocence. Recall that, having discovered Judge Pyncheon's body, he talks Hepzibah into running away with him, and he discovers the train, that marvel of the modern world and then, in a kind of manic joy, talks to a stranger about the future—a future to be reached by just such mechanical means as this. Once Clifford does think of rejoining the mass of humanity from which he has been cut off by the curse that Maule long ago had laid on his family—but by the simple expedient of leaping from the window into the crowd. That is to say, neither he nor Hepzibah can "use" their history, so as not to escape from, but rather to come to grips with, it. When they do find freedom in the end, it is ironically enough a kind of escape and so not wholly satisfactory. But they are old. As is Judge Pyncheon, their tormentor: who in himself projects the curse of history not as it saps moral strength, but as it converts moral strength to brutality. If Clifford is a child, Judge Pyncheon is an animal—accumulating property and power, even, we are told, driving his wife to an early death as he has used her thus. It is fitting that he die as he does, perhaps shocked into his death when he sees Clifford.

In the Romance, the history of the Pyncheon family ends and begins again. It ends because Maule's curse descends on the family for (presumably) the last time. It begins because the sin of the family is exposed, expiated, and the non-Pyncheon world is accepted for what it is: perhaps for the better because those who survive take into it their knowledge of their own history and both the capacity and the determination not to resort to type. Thus, as I have said, the crucial figures are Phoebe and Holgrave.

Holgrave is the New American, we are told, who has been everything and almost everywhere; interested in radical ideas; often cold in his rationalism; determined, since he is convinced that Maule's curse will inevitably work its way with the Pyncheons, to be merely an observer. As daguerreotypist, he is like that mirror in the Pyncheon household that reflects everything. He is also a historian of a sort—as his telling Phoebe the story of Alice Pyncheon and Matthew Maule shows. He is aloof. It never seems to occur to him that he has, in his capacity to mesmerize, himself inherited the sin of his own family. But he is saved by his integrity—his sense of his own "identity" and "individuality," to use Hawthorne's words. And he resists the temptation to mesmerize Phoebe. Both are products of his not being able, at first, to take history, his own and the Pyncheons', into account. At the end, he is able to do so, thus to confirm and consolidate the present by sealing it to the past. And in his actions we see, for the first time in Hawthorne's fiction, a future, or the beginning of a future—a future actualized.

He marries Phoebe, of course. In the end, Hawthorne's capacity to perfect the Romance, to carry it all the way through, depends on his capacity to make us accept Phoebe. I am now persuaded—against the force of much critical opinion—that Hawthorne does manage to do so, if only we grant him that the actualization of the future in the Romance is something of which we are—quite properly in terms of the dialectic of the Romance—to glimpse only the beginning. Phoebe is a prelapsarian Eve—or almost; a Pyncheon who has enough non-Pyncheon blood in her at once to love and to reject her past. For all her goodness—indeed, because of all her goodness—she needs the experience Hawthorne projects for her to begin to mature, to a acquire a level and a mode of experience analogous to Holgrave's, through marriage to become that ripened woman whom Hawthorne in his deepest heart of hearts desiderated if not desired. In the scheme of *The House of the Seven Gables*, desideration has to be, therefore is, enough.[3] There is yet to

3. Writing from Liverpool to his publisher William D. Ticknor 17 February 1854, Hawthorne remarks: "Those are admirable poems of Mrs. Howe's [Julia Ward Howe's *Passion Flowers* (1854), a book that was published anonymously but whose authorship was widely known]. It seems to me to let out a whole history of domestic unhappiness. What a strange propensity it is in these scribbling women to make show of their hearts, as well as their heads, upon your counter, for anybody to pry into that chooses! However, I, for one, am much obliged to the lady, and esteem her beyond all comparison the first of American poetesses. What does her husband think of it?" Having asked Ticknor sometime in September 1854 to send a copy of *Passion Flowers* to Richard Monckton Miles, as one of a "half a dozen good American books" recently published, he subsequently wrote Monckton Miles 13 November 1845: " 'Passion Flowers' are by a very beautiful woman . . . and are certainly more passionate than most husbands would find agreeable. I think we have produced no better poetry than some of her verses." On 19 January 1855 he wrote Ticknor the (now too famous) letter on the "d----d mob of scribbling women." Then on 2 February 1855 he again wrote Ticknor to make amends for his previous "vituperation on female authors." He remarked that he had admired Fanny Fern's (Sara Payson Willis Parton's) *Ruth Hall* and continued: "The woman writes as if the devil was in her; and that is the only condition under which a woman ever writes anything worth reading. Generally, women write like emasculated men, and are only to be distinguished from male authors by greater feebleness and folly; but when they throw off the restraints of decency, and come before the public stark naked, as it were—then their books are sure to possess character and value." (I quote from copy-texts of the letters as they are to be printed in the Centenary Edition.) Setting Hester, Zenobia, and Miriam over against Little Pearl, Phoebe, and Hilda—not to say Sophia Hawthorne over against Elizabeth Hawthorne (passive wife against aggressive sister)—we might well consider these passages. Further, we might well put Hawthorne's problem (as I take it) of desideration as against desire in the context of such investigations as Gloria Erlich's *Family Themes and Hawthorne's Fiction: The Tenacious Web* (Rutgers: Rutgers University Press, 1984), Nancy F. Cott's *The Bonds of Womanhood: "Woman's Sphere" in New England, 1780-1835* (New Haven: Yale University Press, 1977), and Carroll Smith-Rosenberg's "Sex as Symbol in Victorian America," *Prospects* 5 (1980):51-70. On Fanny Fern and *Ruth Hall*, see Ann Douglas Wood, "The 'Scribbling Women' and Fanny Fern: Why Women Wrote," *American Quarterly* 23 (1971):3-24. *Passion Flowers* and *Ruth Hall* in fact differ from the mass of poetry and fiction produced by the "scribbling women" not in their style and rhetoric but in their argument and plotting, in which feminine self-assertiveness marvelously perfects itself, exhausts itself.

come—perhaps in the history of Phoebe's and Holgrave's marriage—
that "brighter period, when the world should have grown ripe for it, in
Heaven's own time, [when] a new truth would be revealed in order to
establish the whole relation between man and woman on a surer ground
of mutual happiness." The words I quote are reported, so Hawthorne
tells us in the "Conclusion" to *The Scarlet Letter*, as the "assurances"
that Hester to her dying day gave to those women who sought her
advice.

In their union, Holgrave and Phoebe—witnesses to their own history—profit from its lessons, mature, and so begin to save one another.
Thus the dialectic of the Romance. In their union—which is that of
two young Americans who have borne the weight of their past while at
the same time being touched by and drawn to the variegated life of the
present—in their union lies the promise of the actualization of the
future. In them—as in the end they are found capable of making and
being made by the life that surrounds them—lies Hawthorne's
expression of his sense at once of the burden of history and the hope of
community, his sense of the present.

We are told, as they tell each other, that they have learned the proper
lessons. Willy-nilly Phoebe, "the flower of Eden," grows. And
Holgrave discovers that he cannot be merely an onlooker if he is really to
"use" the history at whose working out he looks on. What issues is this
simple, straightforward exchange between them:

> "How can you love a simple girl like me?" asked Phoebe, compelled
> by his earnestness to speak. "You have many, many thoughts, with
> which I should try in vain to sympathize. And I—I, too—have tenden-
> cies with which you would sympathize as little. This is less matter. But
> I have not enough scope to make you happy."

Ruth Hall in particular is a nineteenth-century Doppelgängerin of Hester Prynne and
her peers. But then, the scribbling women were but imitating an earlier (and continuing) mob of scribbling men—Hawthorne himself, who in *Fanshawe* (1828) and in the
regularly produced sketches he put into his collection of short pieces, having ventured
to be one of them. When in our current puzzlement we put together, as regards
Hawthorne, what we know of biography, ideology, convention, reader response,
personal and social commitment, and talent, we must for the time being—in our
historicist position—rest puzzled and try to refrain from, for example, the know-
nothingism of Jane Tompkins, "Masterpiece Theatre: The Politics of Hawthorne's
Literary Reputation," *Sensational Designs: The Cultural Work of American Fiction,
1790-1860* (New York: Oxford University Press, 1985), pp. 3-39. That is, we must
know the *primary* facts of the case.

"You are my only possibility of happiness!" answered Holgrave. "I have no faith in it, except as you bestow it on me!"

"And then—I am afraid!" continued Phoebe, shrinking towards Holgrave, even while she told him so frankly the doubts with which he affected her. "You will lead me out of my own quiet path. You will make me strive to follow you where it is pathless. I cannot do so. It is not my nature. I shall sink down and perish."

"Ah Phoebe!" exclaimed Holgrave, with almost a sigh, and a smile that was burdened with thought. "It will be far otherwise than as you forebode. The world owes its onward impulse to men ill at ease. The happy man inevitably confines himself within ancient limits. I have a presentiment that, hereafter, it will be my lot to set out trees, to make fences,—perhaps, even in due time, to build a house for another generation,—in a word, to conform myself to laws, and the peaceful practice of society."

And later when Holgrave (at once ill at ease and happy) speaks of a new house he would build, he speaks—carrying on the vital metaphor of The House of the Seven Gables itself—of a stone, not a wooden, house. As he says, "Then, every generation of the family might have altered the interior, to suit its own taste and convenience; while the exterior, through the lapse of years, might have been adding venerableness to its original beauty, and thus giving that impression of permanence which I consider essential to the happiness of any one moment!" Thus the historical dynamism of the Romance is resolved in Holgrave's and Phoebe's persons, as, in the present, accepting the past, they can envisage the future.

As that dynamism has its "effective operation" on Holgrave and Phoebe, so it must have its dynamism on us, as Hawthorne's readers. In great part of course that operation is worked through our being bid to assent to the perfection of the Romance as it is given its ending in their union. But it also is worked directly on us, as at one crucial point Hawthorne in fact addresses and involves us directly. I refer to that chapter ironically called "Governor Pyncheon"—in which we are to contemplate the body of Judge Pyncheon, now dead, as he sits in the chair in which the original Pyncheon was first given blood to drink. This chapter is to The House of the Seven Gables as "The Whiteness of the Whale" chapter is to Moby-Dick. In it, Hawthorne addresses the reader directly, so as to capture him for the present. This is what he had done (but only by way of preparation) in the Custom House preface to *The Scarlet Letter* and what he anticipates doing, forewarns us that he will do, in the preface to *The House of the Seven Gables*. But now the address, and also the capture, is integral to the Romance itself. Inexorably, Hawthorne makes us consider all that Judge Pyncheon was, could have been, wanted to be, has become. We cannot draw back, even if we would. With Hawthorne, we appeal to Judge Pyncheon to be up and doing; for we know how much he has to do, what an important man he is, that in a way he is not a bad man. In a way. Dead, he contemplates—or rather we contemplate—the richness and variety, the plenitude, of life in the present as it absorbs life in the past. And in the end, in the next-to-last paragraph of the chapter, we must recall, we watch fascinated while a "common house fly . . . which has smelt out Governor Pyncheon [he wanted so much to be more than Judge] . . . alights, now on his forehead, now on his chin, and now, Heaven help us! is choosing over the bridge of his nose, towards the would-be chief magistrate's wide-open eyes. Canst thou not brush the fly away? Art thou too weak, that wast so powerful! Not brush away a fly? Art thou too sluggish? Thou man, that hadst so many busy projects yesterday! Art thou too weak, that wast so powerful! Not brush away a fly? Nay, then, we give thee up!"

Thus, I venture to say, Hawthorne directly addresses us toward the end of assuring that we too are involved in the "effective operation" of the Romance. We hear a fly buzz when Judge Pyncheon dies. Hawthorne's sense of the present, derived from and built upon his sense of the past, becomes not only Clifford's, Hepzibah's, Holgrave's, and Phoebe's, not only Hawthorne's indeed, but also ours. Thus what I have called the perfection of the Romance.

One of Hawthorne's contemporaries, perhaps close friends, understood that perfection and its significance for American letters too. We should recall that, in effect, the most powerful contemporary review of *The House of the Seven Gables*—one that was never published as such but was sent as a letter to Hawthorne—is Herman Melville's. Here is, in part, the most celebrated passage in the letter, which dates April 1851. It comes right after Melville has praised the chapter called "Governor Pyncheon":

> There is a certain tragic phase of humanity which, in our opinion, was never more powerfully embodied than by Hawthorne. We mean

the tragicalness of human thought in its own unbiased, native, and profounder workings. We think that into no recorded mind has the intense feeling of the visible truth ever entered more deeply than into this man's. By visible truth, we mean the apprehension of the absolute condition of present things as they strike the eye of the man who fears them not, though they do their worst to him. . . .

There is the grand truth about Nathaniel Hawthorne. He says no! in thunder; but the Devil himself cannot make him say yes. For all men who say yes, lie; and all men who say no,—why, they are in the happy condition of judicious unincumbered travellers in Europe; they cross the frontiers into Eternity with nothing but a carpet-bag—that is to say, the Ego.[4]

Interpreters of Hawthorne have been a little hard put to apply this passage *in toto* to *The House of the Seven Gables*. I do not see why. For, above all, in the Romance Hawthorne would indeed have all—himself, his protagonists, and his readers—face up to the absolute condition of present things and show how those who cannot do so must necessarily be destroyed, as are Clifford Pyncheon and the Judge. For the absolute condition of present things, when contemplated by those who fear them not, derives in crucial part from the condition of past things. Yet even so, it would not be enough to acquiesce, passively to give in. For a condition of *present* things is that, ineluctably linked as they are with past things, they move into the future. One says NO! in thunder, so to say yes, perhaps only in a whisper, yes to the future. Living in the present entails the willingness and ability to move into the future. Thus in the dialectic of *The House of the Seven Gables*, the union of Phoebe and Holgrave is altogether necessary—"a fine stroke" Melville called it in the letter from which I have quoted. This is the yes, however muted, however putative, that must necessarily come after the thunderous NO in which Hawthorne, on behalf of Phoebe and Holgrave, must reject Clifford, Judge Pyncheon, even Hepzibah.

I am persuaded that after some twenty years of saying NO, Hawthorne, in *The House of the Seven Gables*, was able to say Yes—Yes, not in thunder, but as it should be, in love and in hope, even in charity. *The House of the Seven Gables*, then, is the Romance that, at the culmination of his career, was (in Hawthorne's words to Bridge) "proper and

---

4. *Letters*, ed. M. R. Davis and W. H. Gilman (New Haven: Yale University Press, 1960), pp. 124-25.

natural" for him to write. I have tried to suggest the proper and natural way for us to read and understand it.

1975/1986

5

DAY-DREAM AND FACT:
THE IMPORT OF
THE BLITHEDALE ROMANCE

1

Much of the difficulty we have with *The Blithedale Romance* inevitably derives from the fact of its matrix in Hawthorne's participation in the Brook Farm venture. Granting even his prefatory disclaimers about the relationship of the romance to its "origins" in his experience, we still must insist that the book is an "anti-utopia" and consequently feel obliged to demand of it that it should have qualities of exact and exacting sociocultural observations appropriate to that "genre"; that it should be less melodramatic and more satirical; that its first-person narrator must be either altogether in control of his narrative or altogether its victim—not, as is the actual case, somewhere between the two postures. Anti-utopian writing, we conclude, should not be all that ambiguous. And in our interpretations of *The Blithedale Romance* we tend on the one hand to second-guess Hawthorne and to demonstrate how much better the book would be were it not so ambiguous in its anti-utopianism, or, on the other, to strain to make a case out for it not as an anti-utopia but as an almost perfected romance of protest against things as they were and are—with Coverdale, not Zenobia, the real suicide in the whole affair.

Surely it is crucial for *The Blithedale Romance* that it grows out of Hawthorne's Brook Farm experience. What is centrally at issue—or should be—is his particular interpretation of that experience and his rendering of the interpretation, his sense of the "utopianism" he was doubting, not ours. One way into understanding what he was about is to recall the history of his labors on the text as that history helps clarify the role that his Brook Farm experience played in its conception and composition.[1]

Hawthorne had finished writing *The House of the Seven Gables* in late January 1851, did little or no writing for the next six months, began to worry about a proper subject for his next book in July, and (so his correspondence indicates) abruptly made up his mind. For he wrote to a friend, "When I write another romance, I shall take the Community for a subject, and shall give some of my experiences and observations at Brook Farm." Still, he did not set himself to writing until November and subsequently recorded in his notebook that he wrote the last page of the book he came, after some hesitation, to call *The Blithedale Romance* on 30 April 1852, finished the preface on 1 May, and began to see proof on 14 May. On 2 May he had sent the manuscript to his friend E. P. Whipple, asking for advice. It appears likely that Whipple advised Hawthorne to soften the original ending, so as to give it that measure of "geniality" which he—like Hawthorne's publisher Fields—seems always to have felt Hawthorne's work needed. What is of interest in all this is the evidence it suggests of Hawthorne's abiding professionalism; needing money, he was willing to take marketing advice from those whom he trusted, while still insisting that he must stick to his own last. Meantime Fields was in England and undertook to arrange for publication of *The Blithedale Romance* there; he was successful in negotiating with Chapman and Hall and sold the British rights for 200 pounds, a sum much higher than Hawthorne expected. The English edition appeared shortly before 7 July; the American edition on 14 July. The book sold well at first; but subsequent impressions were small in number. In all, after its initial flurry, the book was no great seller. Fields, particularly disappointed, at one point wrote, "I hope Hawthorne will give us no more Blithedales."

One guesses—and there is a good deal of evidence to make the guess worthwhile—that the book sold well initially not only because it was Hawthorne's but also because its first readers expected—as do its present ones—an insider's account of Brook Farm and its inhabitants. But things just did not work out that way. Hawthorne seems to have begun with the intention of sticking fairly closely to his recollections of Brook Farm, but to have gradually moved away from these recollections in

---

1. What follows derives from my historical introduction to *The Blithedale Romance*, Centenary Edition, 3:xvii-xxvi.

order to give himself the freedom that his gift for the Romance demanded of him. As noted, his first intention was to "take the Community for a subject." A notebook entry of 30 July 1851 shows that he had borrowed some volumes of Fourier, "with a view to my next Romance." The matter was clear enough to Fields, who wrote Bayard Taylor, 5 June 1852, that the scene of Hawthorne's new Romance "is laid at Brook Farm!" (The exclamation point indicates, I think, that Fields too was expecting an insider's account.) Nevertheless, Hawthorne could justifiably write to George W. Curtis, who had belonged to the Community, "Do not read [*The Blithedale Romance*] as if it had anything to do with Brook Farm (which essentially it has not) but merely for its own story and characters." He wrote more bluntly to an unnamed autograph seeker in 1852: "As regards the degree in which the "Blithedale Romance" has a foundation in fact, the preface to the book gives a correct statement."

The preface, then, becomes a critical point of entry—or commencement—for an approach to *The Blithedale Romance*. Claiming that his recollections of Brook Farm are but incidental to his story, Hawthorne is explicit as to his intentions:

> In short, his present concern with the Socialist Community is merely to establish a theatre, a little removed from the highway of ordinary travel, where the creatures of his brain may play their phantasmagorical antics, without exposing them to too close a comparison with the actual events of real lives.

He would claim the privileges of the romancer who needs a "Faery Land, so like the real world, that, in a suitable remoteness, one cannot well tell the difference, but with an atmosphere of strange enchantment, beheld through which the inhabitants have a propriety of their own." It follows that his characters are not to be understood as real Brook Farmers but as types entirely appropriate to a romance: "The self-concentrated Philanthropist; the high-spirited Woman, bruising herself against the narrow limitations of her sex; the weakly Maiden, whose tremulous nerves endow her with Sibylline attributes; the Minor Poet, beginning life with strenuous aspirations which die out with his youthful fervor."

These sentiments and these claims are of course analogous to those in the preface to *The House of the Seven Gables*. And they derive from a problem common to the two romances—indeed, to virtually all of Hawthorne's work after *The Scarlet Letter*: that he set himself increasingly to treating contemporaneous life and so found himself increasingly concerned with the sort of materials that the novel as a literary form had been evolved to comprehend: the experience of life as interesting, demanding, and valuable precisely as it could be conceived of in terms lived through day-to-day. The romancer's problem was in effect to get such perspective on that experience as would free him of the novelist's regular commitment to evoke it in its own terms, so to be in some ultimate sense at least a "realist." Hawthorne's means to this end in *The House of Seven Gables* had been to conceive of himself as a historian whose special knowledge of the history of the Pyncheons gave him a power of psychological perception such that he could function as romancer.

The problem in *The Blithedale Romance*, granting its matrix in Hawthorne's Brook Farm experience, granting his dubiety about that experience (itself quite evident in opinions expressed when he was actually at Brook Farm), is a particularly difficult one. For it is immanently necessary in anti-utopian writings—as in the utopian writings that call them forth—that there be a strong quality of novelistic treatment. This derives from the nature of the utopian enterprise itself, in which revolutionary fantasies are rendered as though realizable in quite concrete, particular, immediate, and realistic terms.

Henry James's contrast of the real and the romantic—especially because it comes in the midst of his lucubrations on Hawthorne—is useful here:

> The real represents to my perception the things we cannot possibly *not* know, sooner or later, in one way or another; it being but one of the accidents of our hampered state, and one of the incidents of their quantity and number, that particular instances have not yet come our way. The romantic stands, on the other hand, for the things that, with all the facilities in the world, all the wealth and all the courage and all the wit and the adventure, we never *can* directly know; the things that can reach us only through the beautiful circuit and subterfuge of our thought and our desire.

Hope for a utopian society may well be rooted in the romantic impulse as James defines it. But its realization, ironically enough, depends upon bringing into full play the realistic impulse. As it were, "particular instances" must not be just generally, exotically, or allegorically desiderated, but rather forced to "come our way"—forced into being in concrete and particular "quantity and number." When what is in question is anti-utopian writing, the burden of the novelistic is all the greater. For then there is a further formal problem, that of satire. (As it has recently been demonstrated, utopia, anti-utopia, and satire are, as literary modes, in their origin and development, as well as in their form and function, integrally related one with another.)[2] Behind James's discomfort with *The Blithedale Romance* in his little book on Hawthorne lie the problems he sets for himself in his later preface to the New York edition of *The American*. And James's discomfort has of course been that of many critics who have come after him. That discomfort is at the root of our difficulty with *The Blithedale Romance*.

2

The primary intention of Hawthorne's preface to *The Blithedale Romance*, then, is to assuage that discomfort and to find a way around that difficulty. Hawthorne is insisting not that we forget about the "real" Brook Farm but rather that we should let ourselves be guided into an acceptance of what he has made out of his experience there:

> This ["Faery Land"] atmosphere is what the American romancer needs. In its absence, the beings of imagination are compelled to show themselves in the same category as actually living mortals; a necessity that generally renders the paint and pasteboard of their composition but too painfully discernible. With the idea of partially obviating this difficulty (the sense of which has always pressed very heavily upon him), the author has ventured to make free with his old, and affectionately remembered home, at BROOK FARM, as being, certainly, the most romantic episode of his own life—essentially a day-dream, and yet a fact—and thus offering an available foothold between fiction and reality. Furthermore, the scene was in good keeping with the personages whom he desired to introduce.

The principal personage so introduced is Miles Coverdale. Hawthorne compounds his formal problem and complicates our comprehending his point of view by introducing Coverdale as a first-person narrator—

2. See particularly Robert Elliott, "Saturnalia, Satire, and Utopia," *The Shape of Utopia: Studies in a Literary Genre* (Chicago: University of Chicago Press, 1970), pp. 3-24.

sometimes unreliable—in whose vocabulary, as Hawthorne creates it for him, terms like "daydream" and its analogues are prime instruments of understanding and interpretation. Hawthorne's critique of Brook Farm, one concludes, is a critique of a daydream made out to be rendered by a daydreamer, a recollection of a fantasy by a compulsive fantast, an anti-utopia told by a failed utopian.

The task accordingly set for the interpreter of *The Blithedale Romance* is to ascertain the particular utopian quality of Blithedale, not of Brook Farm. That quality, in a word, is Arcadian: a version of what A. O. Lovejoy long ago analyzed as Western Man's overwhelming yearning to return to what he was sure must have been an earlier, simpler state of affairs, "soft primitivism"; what we can describe, in psychological terms, as a compulsion to idyllic regression. Hawthorne does have Coverdale and the others—when they are brought to confront this state of affairs—speak ironically, though most often their irony is directed not at themselves but at their fellows, as though each thinks that the other, not himself, is guilty of Arcadianism. Moreover, in the particular case of Coverdale (and the particular case is integral with his being a first-person narrator whose style as thinker is perilously close to that of his creator as it is set forth in the preface), there is evidence of what we might best call a manifest and a latent Arcadianism. In the first instance, Coverdale habitually mocks the utopian aspirations of those at Blithedale, often including himself. In the second instance, however, Hawthorne makes him, all-unknowing, reveal his own regressive qualities; herein he is—especially in the last third of the romance—the arch peeping tom, the voyeur who, hoping to find a means of simplifying his life to the uttermost, longs for an Arcadia beyond the ken of that his fellows are trying to create, an Arcadia of the solitary. It might well be that, in creating Coverdale, Hawthorne was trying to exorcise out of himself a fundamental drive in his own character, as in creating Blithedale and its special society, he was trying to come to grips with a vital portion of his own history. At any rate, what is centrally at issue in *The Blithedale Romance*—what is central to its import—is utopianism as Arcadianism.

The motif is sharply delineated early in the narrative, in chapter 8—"A Modern Arcadia." Coverdale emerges from his sickroom on May Day, and, as the narrative progresses, for the first time begins to see the relationship that obtains among Zenobia, Priscilla, and Hollingsworth.

He finds Zenobia and Priscilla "a Maying together" and, as Hollingsworth appears, realizes how Priscilla is torn between her devotion to the other two. He sees the whole scene as somehow vitalizing and now senses that at Blithedale he can undergo a kind of rebirth:

> My fit of illness had been an avenue between two existences; the low-arched and darksome doorway, through which I had crept out of a life of old conventionalisms, on my hands and knees, as it were, and gained admittance into the freer region that lay beyond. In this respect, it was like death. And, as with death, too, it was good to have gone through it. Not otherwise could I have rid myself of a thousand follies, fripperies, prejudices, habits, and other such worldly dust as inevitably settles upon the crowd along the broad highway, giving them all one sordid aspect, before noontime, however freshly they may have begun their pilgrimage, in the dewy morning. The very substance upon my bones had not been fit to live with, in any better, truer, or more energetic mode than that to which I was accustomed. So it was taken off me and flung aside, like any other worn out or unseasonable garment; and, after shivering a little while in my skeleton, I began to be clothed anew, and much more satisfactorily than in my previous suit. In literal and physical truth, I was quite another man.

And so he is led to meditate on the forces that make Blithedale operative. Above all, he decides, his life and that of his fellows is now no longer artificially ordered, its conventions now being set by the fundamental laws of "Nature." The rationale is the traditional one in Arcadian-primitivistic thought. As "Arcadians," he writes, those at Blithedale—individualists all—are nonetheless not "the pastoral people of poetry and the stage." Rather, they live a "yeoman life." At this point he can afford to be ironic—this time concerning the difficulties confronting Arcadians when they would set themselves to physical labor. The irony, so it develops as the narrative continues, is also sensed by Zenobia and Hollingsworth, whom he reports as being amused at the sight of a minor poet turned yeoman. Hollingsworth at least approves. Coverdale reports him as commenting: "There is at least this good in a life of toil, that it takes the nonsense and fancy-work out of a man, and leaves nothing but what truly belongs to him." At this point, Zenobia accepts Hollingsworth's truth as her own, and Coverdale—now with them a committed Arcadian—does not gainsay them.

Chapter 8 serves as an initial focal point for the Arcadian motifs in

The Blithedale Romance. The motifs, however, are highlighted throughout the romance. In chapter 3, Coverdale recalls his proclaiming his intention to begin writing a new kind of poetry—"true, strong, natural, and sweet, as is the life we are going to lead." In this chapter too he remembers his discovering that Zenobia can be another Eve, as life at Blithedale will not be "artificial." In chapter 4 there is the record of Hollingsworth's declaration that the coming of Priscilla indeed marks a new beginning of things, and in chapter 5 is his insistence that his utopia, his "socialist scheme," will be wholly altruistic. In chapter 5 too there is reported the discussion of the search for a name for the colony; "Utopia," presumably because it calls to mind "artificial" arrangements, is "unanimously scouted down" and Blithedale is agreed upon—all this on an evening when Coverdale must report, with an irony whose full implications he cannot foresee, "How cold an Arcadia was this!" In chapter 9 Coverdale comments that it was in the nature of Blithedale to incline all "to the soft affections of the Golden Age," and later Zenobia is reported as describing events at Blithedale (here again there is an irony whose eventual implications are not foreseen) as the playing out of a "pastoral." In chapter 10 Coverdale says that, in the view of visitors to Blithedale, "we were as poetical as Arcadians, besides being as practical as the hardest-fisted husbandmen in Massachusetts." And so it goes—until toward the end, when in chapter 20 Zenobia, in town, annoyed at Coverdale's spying on her, is reported as speaking of "such Arcadian freedom of falling in love as we lately have enjoyed," and when in chapter 23 Coverdale, looking back, can say only of his earlier Arcadian hopes for his time at Blithedale, "it had enabled me to pass the summer in a novel and agreeable way, had afforded me some grotesque specimens of artificial simplicity."

The movement, as regards the Arcadian motifs, is from naive commitment to amused irony to disillusionment. But there is a degree of ambiguity at all points—an ambiguity deriving in good part from Coverdale's being continually caught between the realms of daydream and fact. The turning point, if it can justifiably be called that, perhaps comes toward the middle of the narrative, in chapter 15, after Coverdale has at long last begun to realize the terrible complications of the relationships among Zenobia, Priscilla, and Hollingsworth. It is in this chapter that Hollingsworth first manifests himself for what he is — single mindedly devoted to his version of utopia, altogether careless of the aspirations of others. In the course of their conversation Coverdale begins to have his doubts about the perdurability of Blithedale and all that it stands for. He sees that death must inevitably come to someone in this Arcadia:

"I wonder, Hollingsworth, who, of all these strong men, and fair women and maidens, is doomed the first to die. Would it not be well, even before we have the absolute need of it, to fix upon a spot for a cemetery? Let us choose the rudest, roughest, most uncultivable spot, for Death's garden-ground; and Death shall teach us to beautify it, grave by grave."

There is portrayed here a crisis (and the chapter is called "A Crisis") not only in Hollingsworth's relationships with his fellows but also in Coverdale's sense of the whole Arcadian enterprise that is Blithedale. But, here again, Hawthorne is writing according to the Arcadian tradition. For this episode derives—whether or not consciously on Hawthorne's part, it is impossible to say—from the traditional "Et in Arcadia ego" topos, in which the presence of death is found to be ineluctable in the Arcadian scheme of things.[3] And the "Et in Arcadia ego" topos is affirmed at almost the very end, in chapter 27, when Coverdale must mediate on the "ugly circumstances" of Zenobia's suicide and of the injury to her body done in the process of recovering it. He somehow cannot believe that Zenobia would have drowned herself if she had realized how indecorous she would have looked in death. For, he writes, "in Zenobia's case there was some tint of the Arcadian affectation that had been visible enough in all our lives, for a few months past."

3

The Arcadian mode was indeed an affectation in Hawthorne's view of things. He has Coverdale, in exhausted retrospect, write of Blithedale in the last, "confessional" chapter: "The experiment, so far as its original projectors were concerned, proved, long ago a failure, first lapsing into Fourierism, and dying, as it well deserved, for this infidelity to its own higher spirit." Hawthorne, indeed, believed wholeheartedly in that "higher spirit," but could nonetheless find it, for people like Coverdale and the rest, an affectation. It was an affecta-

3. The classical study on the topos of course is Erwin Panofsky, "*Et in Arcadia Ego*: Poussin and the Elegiac Tradition," *Meaning in the Visual Arts* (New York: Doubleday, 1955), pp. 295-320.

tion for such as them, because it was a "higher spirit" appropriate only to children. What is centrally involved in *The Blithedale Romance*—what gives it its special import—is Hawthorne's conviction that willy-nilly Coverdale and the rest are acting like children, trying to reduce—or to return—life to terms impossible for adults. Surely Coverdale's voyeurism, including its sexual aspects as his attitude toward Zenobia reveals them, has something to do with his failure to grow up. At this point some historical considerations are again worth noting. *The Blithedale Romance* is a project Hawthorne undertook at that point in his life when at long last he was doing what he had committed himself to do as early as 1838, retelling Greek myths in a style appropriate to children. The chronology is important.[4] On 1 January 1851, Hawthorne finished *The House of the Seven Gables*. On 7 April 1851, he reported to a correspondent that he was planning *A Wonder-Book*. On 3 May 1851, he reported that *A Wonder-Book* was in fact designed. On 15 July 1851, *A Wonder-Book* was in his publisher Fields's hands. On 24 July 1851, he reported that he had decided to write a book based on his Brook Farm experiences. On 8 November 1851, *A Wonder-Book* was published. Around 23 November 1851, he reported that he had begun to write the book that became *The Blithedale Romance*. On 2 May 1852, he sent the manuscript of *The Blithedale Romance* to Whipple. On 8 June 1852, he reported that he was thinking about writing a continuation of *A Wonder-Book* (this became *Tanglewood Tales*). He was stalled in this enterprise subsequently, because he agreed to write Franklin Pierce's campaign biography and then involved himself in the campaign itself. In November 1852, with Pierce elected, he knew that he would get the consulship at Liverpool; and on 15 March 1853, he could report that he was working on the continuation of *A Wonder-Book*. *Tanglewood Tales* was published in England and the United States in August 1853.

The point of the chronologizing is to emphasize the fact that *The Blithedale Romance* was written at a time when Hawthorne was most deeply concerned to demonstrate that Arcadianism was quite properly a stage in the development of the child's life. Both *A Wonder-Book* and *Tanglewood Tales* center on that notion. Hawthorne has a young collegian, Eustace Bright, retell Greek myths from a child's perspective. More important to the present argument, he is persuaded that the

4. What follows derives from my historical introduction to Hawthorne's writings for children, Centenary Edition, 6:287-311.

myths, as he has them retold, are pure not only from the child's point of view but also from a historical point of view. Hawthorne went to standard learned sources, took the myths as they had come down to him, but felt bound to take into account the fact that over the ages they had accreted to themselves the complications and corruptions of adult life—complications and corruptions that he made clear were inevitable but nonetheless were not integral to the myths in their "pure" state. This is yet another version of his obsession with *felix culpa*.

The best summary of his view occurs in the preface to *Tanglewood Tales*, in which he speaks in his own person:

> Eustace told me that these myths were the most singular things in the world, and that he was invariably astonished, whenever he began to relate one, by the readiness with which it adapted itself to the childish purity of his auditors. The objectionable characteristics seem to be a parasitical growth, having no essential connection with the original fable. . . . When the first poet or romancer told these marvellous legends (such was Eustace Bright's opinion), it was still the Golden Age. Evil had never yet existed; and sorrow, misfortune, crime, were mere shadows which the mind fancifully created for itself, as a shelter against too sunny realities—or, at most, but prophetic dreams, to which the dreamer himself did not yield a waking credence. Children are now the only representatives of the men and women of that happy era; and therefore it is that we must raise the intellect and the fancy to the level of childhood, in order to re-create the original myths.

Hawthorne is here eulogizing the sort of world that he perforce treated dyslogistically in *The Blithedale Romance*. For the Arcadian world of Blithedale is essentially—and for Hawthorne's purposes, inappropriately—a child's world, not the sort of utopia of which Emerson wrote so cheerfully in "New England Reformers" (1844): "What a fertility of projects for the salvation of the world!" Rather the world of Blithedale is one to which all concerned willy-nilly regress in their desperate attempt to find a place where what they take to be their gifts and commitments can be realized. It is a Land of Cockaigne in which the Identity Crisis (the critic needs the concepts of ego psychology if he is to be a proper literary historian) can be forever postponed.

Early in the romance, Hawthorne writes: "As for Zenobia, there was a glow in her cheeks that made me think of Pandora, fresh from Vulcan's workshop, and full of the celestial warmth by dint of which he had tempered and moulded her." In *A Wonder-Book* Hawthorne retells the Pandora myth in a story called "The Paradise of Children." Pandora, in this piece, is a child, as is Epithemeus, her husband in traditional versions of the story. She fusses at length over the mysterious box that Mercury has left, does not realize that her existence is idyllic, and finally opens the box, releasing a multitude of evils on the world, but also releasing Hope. In the middle of the story, Hawthorne comments thus on his Pandora:

> It might have been better for Pandora if she had had a little work to do, or anything to employ her mind upon, so as not to be so constantly thinking of [opening the box]. But children led so easy a life, before any Troubles came into the world, that they really had a great deal too much leisure. . . . When life is all sport, toil is the real play.

Those in residence at Blithedale, it will be recalled, do in fact "toil, but, once they discover that toil is in fact not play, not enthusiastically." What they *really* wish, Hawthorne is suggesting, is that regressive state of life wherein they will be free to realize themselves in a way the conditions of life lived day-to-day in society will not allow. With the exception of Zenobia—and this is what makes her, as James first pointed out, Hawthorne's most realized woman—they have rejected the option of adjusting their fantasies to the exigencies of life lived in the world proper. She is the exception, because such an option does not altogether exist for her. But she is nonetheless not quite right, since she could have changed her name and her life-style to that, not of Margaret Fuller, but of Elizabeth or Mary Peabody. She remains, however, a passionate *Sophia* Peabody. And that is her tragedy, the only one in *The Blithedale Romance*. The rest is pathos.

It could have been more. Hawthorne, I am persuaded, did not have sufficient perspective on his own commitment to the notion that childhood, however Arcadian, was also a stage in growing up and into the world, a world which could not be that of the romance. Still, I think the tone of the book—mocking in its irony, not satirical—is justified by its intention and its import. My own historical fantasy as regards the place of *The Blithedale Romance* in Hawthorne's oeuvre is that the young collegian, Eustace Bright, who tells the stories in *A Wonder-Book* and *Tanglewood Tales*, finished college, tried his hand at literature, could not bring himself to face the practicalities of the life of the writer as his friend Nathaniel Hawthorne had done, with Hawthorne went to Brook Farm, and never recovered from the experience, precisely because the experience was for him, as it was not for Hawthorne, an abiding fact rather than a kind of daydream. Later—as I reconstruct the inside story of *The Blithedale Romance*—he recounted his adventures, hopes, and aspirations to Hawthorne and agreed that his friend might tell them, if only his name were changed. From Bright to Coverdale. Any literary historian—with some etymological training—would understand.

1975

6

WHITMAN JUSTIFIED:
THE POET IN 1855

The tenth of the "Chants Democratic" in the 1860 *Leaves of Grass* reads as follows:

> Historian! you who celebrate bygones!
> You have explored the outward, the surface of the races—the
>   life that has exhibited itself,
> You have treated man as the creature of politics,
>   aggregates, rulers, and priests;
> But now I also, arriving, contribute something:
> I, an habitué of the Alleghanies, treat man as he is in the
>   influences of Nature, in himself, in his own
>   inalienable rights,
> Advancing, to give the spirit and the traits of new
>   Democratic ages, myself, personally,
> (Let the future behold them all in me—Me, so puzzling and
>   contradictory—Me, a Manhattanese, the most loving and
>   arrogant of men;)
> I do not tell the usual facts, proved by records and
>   documents,
> What I tell, (talking to every born American,) requires no
>   further proof than he or she who will hear me, will
>   furnish, by silently meditating alone;
> I press the pulse of the life that has hitherto seldom
>   exhibited itself, but has generally sought concealment,
>   (the great pride of man, in himself,)
> I illuminate the feelings, faults, yearnings, hopes—I have
>   come at last, no more ashamed nor afraid;
> Chanter of Personality, outlining a history yet to be,
> I project the ideal man, the American of the future

Working over this poem as he was preparing what came to be the 1867

edition of *Leaves of Grass*, Whitman found it troublesome.[1] He decided
to reject the poem, then changed his mind three times, finally putting
into the 1867 *Leaves of Grass* the relatively bare version in which, virtually unchanged, it has been preserved, entitled "To a Historian," as
one of the "Inscriptions" poems of the 1891-1892 *Leaves of Grass*:

> You who celebrate bygones,
> Who have explored the outward, the surfaces of races, the
>   life that has exhibited itself,
> Who have treated of man as the creature of politics,
>   aggregates, rules and priests,
> I, habitan of the Alleghanies, treating of him as he is in
>   himself in his own rights,
> Pressing the pulse of the life that has seldom exhibited
>   itself, (the great pride of man in himself,)
> Chanter of Personality, outlining what is yet to be,
> I project the history of the future.

Comparing the poem in its final form to its first version, Harold
Blodgett and Sculley Bradley, the editors of the Comprehensive
Reader's Edition of *Leaves of Grass*, note that the first version is
"inflated."[2] The remark is correct but not to the point. The point is
that both versions manifest a compulsion, increasingly evident in Whitman from 1860 onward, to write small poems explanatory of his intentions, pocket compendia of his poetics as it were, so that they may serve
as our way into understanding his attitude toward his substantial concerns as the larger, justifiably inflated (and conflated) poems project
them. Two of the lines dropped in the 1867 version of "To a Historian"
indicate that in the 1860 *Leaves of Grass* Whitman would (to use a later
term of his) "vivify" the past in such a way that his readers, assenting to
it in deep contemplation, might (to use one of *our* terms for "vivify")
introject it, or their sense of it. The dropped lines are:

> I do not tell the usual facts, proved by records and
>   documents,
> What I tell, (talking to every born American,) requires no

---

1. I follow both the facsimile of Whitman's *Blue Book* and the analysis of it given in
Arthur Golden's absolutely invaluable *Walt Whitman's Blue Book*, 2 vols. (New York:
New York University Press, 1968), esp. 2:181-82. The poem was given its final form in
the 1871 *Leaves of Grass*.
2. *Leaves of Grass* (New York: New York University Press, 1965), p. 4.

further proof than he or she who will hear me, will
furnish, by silently meditating alone[.]

A condition of his reader's understanding Whitman's "outlining a history yet to be" is accepting it as in fact—the sort of fact, worked
through in meditation—it has actually been. I think, then, that it is not
fortuitous that the early Whitman in particular has proved so amenable
to the sort of understanding deriving from ego psychology, with its
special emphasis on the very historicity of human experience. For in
fact—the sort of fact *I* intend to work through here in meditation—the
early Whitman himself was possessed of that sort of understanding.[3]
The early Whitman, I must emphasize. For it is the early Whitman—
he of the 1855, '56, and '60 *Leaves of Grass*—whom we must read,
would we, through his work, achieve that sort of understanding. The
moments are there. They are few. But I believe they are precious.

The greatest of them is in the 1855 "Song of Myself" and is preserved
in the 1856 and 1860 versions. In what he came to number section 34 of
the poem, Whitman continues to seek for the sort of identifications he
had begun to seek starting in section 26.[4] But now they are what comprise his and his reader's history. In section 34 he gives a graphic account
of the fall of the Alamo, an account pretty much kept through all subsequent editions of *Leaves of Grass*. In the next section occurs the account
of the battle between the *Bon Homme Richard* and the *Serapis*. The 1855
version begins:

> Did you read in the seabooks of the oldfashioned frigate-
> fright?
> Did you learn who won by the light of the moon and stars?

By 1891-1892 this had been changed to:

> Would you hear of an old-time sea-fight?
> Would you learn who won by the light of the moon and stars?
> List to the yarn, as my grandmother's father the sailor told
> it to me.

The shift from "Did" to "Would," preterit to conditional, per-fected

---

3. See Erik Erikson: "historical actuality also points to the available resources
which permit transformation of the past into a future of more inclusive identities"
(*Insight and Responsibility* [New York: W. W. Norton, 1964], p. 206).
4. See my outline of the "argument" of the poem in *The Continuity of American
Poetry* (Princeton: Princeton University Press, 1961), p. 74.

to pro-fected, and from the emphasis upon learning from reading to learning from listening, signals the attenuation of the importance of historicity—the past vivified, documents silently meditated on—in Whitman's creative sensibility. The changes, except for small stylistic details, were for the greater part made for the 1867 version of the poem. So it is for the rest of sections 35 and 36, with section 34 the explicitly historical portions of "Song of Myself." The account of the battle in the 1855 version begins directly: "Our foe was no skulk in his ship, I tell you[.]" To this line in 1867 Whitman added "(said he,)"—thus again emphasizing listening as against reading, communal oral tradition as against individually sought out historical documents, and, most important for the sense of historicity, passive fascination as against active mediation—"silently meditating alone." The shift in effect is intensified in what follows, in which 1855 version verbs in the past tense are shifted to the present. Vivification in the latter versions is earned too easily and becomes a matter of mere liveliness. The past becomes the present, not as the 1855 version of "To a Historian" would demand, through historical understanding, but through a species of journalism. If Whitman thought that he was increasing his epic scope by the use of the historical present, he sorely misunderstood the profound difficulty of the proper use of that technique, which is persuasive only in a society in which a preexistent myth, to which reader (more likely auditor) and poet are both committed, assures in advance of the poem that a past action is/remains literally present. In 1855 Whitman understood that this was an effect (with its corresponding affect) that had to be *achieved*, since it was not/could not be *guaranteed*. And so, in the 1855 version, it goes through the end of section 36:

> Stretched and still lay the midnight,
> Two great hulls motionless on the breast of darkness,
> Our vessel riddled and slowly sinking . . . . preparations
>   to pass to the one we had conquered,
> The captain on the quarter deck coldly giving his orders
>   through a countenance white as a sheet,
> Near by the corpse of the child that served in the cabin,
> The dead face of an old salt with long white hair and
>   carefully curled whiskers,
> The flames spite of all that could be done flickering aloft
>   and below,
> The huskey voices of the two or three officers yet too fit

for duty,
Formless stacks of bodies and bodies by themselves . . . .
    dabs of flesh upon the masts and spars,
The cut of cordage and dangle of rigging . . . . the slight
    shock of the soothe of the waves,
Black and impassive guns, and litter of powder-parcels, and
    the strong scent,
Delicate sniffs of the seabreeze . . . . smells of sedgy
    grass and fields by the shore . . . . death messages
    given in charge to survivors,
The hiss of the surgeon's knife and the gnawing teeth of his
    saw,
The wheeze, the cluck, the swash of falling blood . . . .
    the short wild scream, the long dull tapering groan,
These so . . . . irretrievable.

By 1867 the verbs had been shifted to present tense, so that the beautifully compulsive sequence of noun-phrases no longer, as we read these lines, is presented—through syntactic art, foregrounded into our consciousness. By 1867, that is to say, the poet does not face the problem of moving us with him from evocation of the past to silent meditation in the present. For he has never really left the present, even in imagination. In 1855 the problem is confronted and beautifully solved; this is the passage that immediately follows in 1855 the passage just quoted and is preserved with quite minor (but, in my opinion, still somewhat debilitating) changes through 1860:

O Christ! My fit is mastering me!
What the rebel said gaily adjusting his throat to the rope-
    noose,
What the savage said at the stump, his eye-sockets empty,
    his mouth spirting whoops and defiance,
What stills the traveler come to the vault at Mount Vernon,
What sobers the Brooklyn boy as he looks down the shores of
    the Wallabout and remembers the prison ships,
What burnt the gums of the redcoat at Saratoga when he
    surrendered his brigades,
These become mine and me every one, and they are but little,
I become as much more as I like.

I become any presence or truth of humanity here,
And see myself in prison shaped like another man,
And feel the dull unintermitted pain.

This passage, in which present and past are inextricably implicated one in the other, was dropped in the 1867 version. The evidence of Whitman's holograph reworking of the 1860 version shows that he needed a transition to what would follow, yet he could not bring himself to preserve the sense of the historicity in what he had written for the 1855 version and had kept substantially intact through 1860. At one point, so the holograph reworking shows, he proposed to himself to substitute for the passage just quoted:

> The days I live[,] the passions immense,
> The bloody vindictive battles, with thousands falling, or
> throes of peace or war[.]

As though quite simply to sum up, so to manage a least common denominator sense of the past. In any case, what Whitman eventually wrote, so to eliminate all but the final line of the rejected passage I have quoted, was:

> You laggards there on guard! Look to your arms!
> In at the conquer'd doors they crowd! I am possess'd!
> Embody all the presences outlaw'd or suffering,
> See myself in prison shaped like another man,
> And feel the dull unintermitted pain.

Possessed by himself in the acting, or failing to possess or be possessed by the historical other. So much, then, for that great hope:

> I do not tell the usual facts, proved by records and
> documents,
> What I tell, (talking to every born American,) requires no
> further proof than he or she who will hear me, will
> furnish, by silently meditating alone[.]

That Whitman was in 1855-1860 and somewhat beyond quite aware of what he has about, as regards understanding what I would call the historic component of our experience, is variously manifest. There is, in the 1860 *Leaves of Grass*, the nineteenth of the "Chants Democratic," in which he insists that the "paged fables in the libraries, [which he] neither accept[s] nor reject[s]," must be made to comport with the life and institutions of "the average man of to-day." An entry in his *Primer of Words* (from the 1850s but not published until 1904, in a too rigorously edited version by Horace Traubel) reads:

Kosmos-words, Words of the *Free Expansion of Thought, History, Chronology, Literature*, are showing themselves, with foreheads muscular necks and breasts.—These gladden me!—I put my arms around them—touch my lips to them.—the past hundred centuries have confided much to me, yet they mock me, frowning.—I think I am done with many of the words of the past hundred centuries.—I am mad that their poems, bibles, words, still rule and represent the earth, and are not superseded. But why do I say so?—I must not,—will not, be impatient.—[5]

Emerson would appear to be a primary source, as in so much of the initial and initiating Whitman, as in this definition of this tendency, or mood, or mode. For Emerson, history is not the actual biography of great men but rather the radically possible autobiography of all men. Thus he wrote in "History," from the first series of *Essays*:

There is one mind common to all individual men. Every man is an inlet to the same and to all of the same. He that is once admitted to the right of reason is made a freeman of the whole estate. What Plato has thought, he may think; what a saint has felt, he may feel; what at any time has befallen any man, he can understand. Who hath access to this universal mind is a party to all that is or can be done, for this is the only sovereign agent.

* * *

We sympathize in the great moments of history, in the great discoveries, the great resistances, the great prosperities of men; because there law was enacted, the sea was searched, the land was found, or the blow was struck, *for us*, as we ourselves in that place would have done or applauded.

* * *

These hints, dropped as it were from sleep and night, let us use in broad day. The student is to read history actively and not passively; to esteem his own life the text, and books the commentary. Thus compelled, the Muse of history will utter oracles, as never to those who do not respect themselves. I have no expectations that any man will read history aright who thinks that what was done in any remote age, by men whose names have resounded far, has any deeper sense than what he is doing to-day.

5. *The Collected Writings: Daybooks and Notebooks*, ed. William White, 3 vols. (New York: New York University Press, 1978), 3:739.

In some historians and philosophers of history in the nineteenth century, the mood was indeed a mode, with a logic of its own. The great
proponent of this mode was Wilhelm Dilthey (1833-1911), whose self-set
task as a post-Kantian was to construct a critique of *historical* reason.
Here is Dilthey, in a posthumously published fragment, on what the
task would entail:

> [Historical] understanding is a rediscovery of the I in the Thou; mind
> rediscovers itself on higher and higher levels of systematic connection;
> this identity of mind in the I, in the Thou, in every subject within a
> community, in every system of culture, and finally in the totality of
> mind and of world history, makes possible the joint result of the various
> operations performed in the human studies. The knowing subject is
> here one with its object, and this object is the same on all levels of
> objectification. If by this procedure we come to recognize the objec-
> tivity of the world of mind built up in the subject's consciousness, we
> must then go on to ask how much this can contribute to the solution of
> the problem of knowledge in general.[6]

Whitman was not one to be troubled about the solution of the problem of knowledge in particular, much less in general, nor for that matter
was Emerson. Their way was to postulate solutions to problems just
before they encountered them. My point, however, is that Whitman,
with Emerson, did encounter a problem, the Diltheyan solution to
which has tempted philosophers of history into our own time. If in
quoting Dilthey as a gloss on Emerson I would seem to want to involve
Whitman in philosophical issues beyond this ken, then instead I would
recall an earlier, quite fundamental statement of the mood, rather than
one of the mode: "That which hath been is now; and that which is to be
hath already been; and God requireth that which is past." The King
James version of these words from Revelations 3:16 is perhaps clarified
in the Revised Standard version: "That which is, already has been; that
which is to be, already has been, and God seeks what has been driven
away."
     In any case, as my animadversions on the 1867 *Leaves of Grass* have
indicated, Whitman—like Emerson, in fact—could not hold on to this
historic credo as mood or mode. An entry from a presumably 1850s

6. Dilthey quoted by H. A. Hodges, *Wilhelm Dilthey: An Introduction* (London:
Routledge and Kegan Paul, 1944), p. 114.

notebook indicates Whitman's awareness of just how difficult it would
be to maintain his initial all-out Emersonianism:

> Walt Whitman stands to-day in the midst of the American people, a
> promise, a preface, an overture, a . . . . Will he fulfill the half-distinct
> half-indistinct promise?—Many do not understand him, but there are
> others, a few, who do understand him. Will he justify the great proph-
> ecy of Emerson? Or will he too, like thousands of others, flaunt out
> one bright commencement, the result of gathered powers, only to sink
> back exhausted—or to give himself up to the seduction of.[7]

Whitman's position on these matters, 1855 to 1860, like Emerson's,
was in fact radical and was set against the received view of the way
Americans should view their past. In 1850, reviewing—really edi-
torializing upon—the "conservative" Richard Hildreth's *History of the
United States*, the "liberal" Theodore Parker could say: "As the history
of Christianity must be written by a Christian who can write from
within, the history of art by a man with an artistic soul, so must the
history of America be written by a democrat—we mean one who puts
man before the accidents of man, valuing his permanent nature more
than the transient results of his history."[8] It is precisely the indestruc-
tibility of "the accidents of man" and the intransigence of his history on
which Emerson and Whitman both, for a time, could insist. The Civil
War and its discontents intervened, of course. And Whitman—Emerson too, I think, but that is another story—was swamped in the long
run by "liberal" conclusions like this one from 1862:

> Those who have regarded this war from an elevated point of view, who
> have taken in all the causes which led to it, must see and feel that the
> great principle of free labor—of fully developed, vigorous, and cheerful
> industry, with its inseparable aids, science and art—involve far more
> than its most hopeful partisans have claimed. When matured, they
> must bring forth new forms of art and literature, new phases of culture.
> I do not believe with many that in this age of labor, industry and utili-
> tarianism are killing beauty and poetry. On the contrary, I see that they
> form the transition stage to a higher art and poetry than the world has
> ever known, and that through their dusty, steam-engine whirling real-
> ism, society will yet attain to a naturalism, or a living and working in

7. *The Collected Writings: Daybooks and Notebooks*, 3:779. The hiatuses are Whitman's, although I have edited the verbatim transcript for my purposes.

8. *Theodore Parker: An Anthology*, ed. H. S. Commager (Boston: Beacon Press,
1960), p. 212.

nature, more direct, fresher, and braver, than history has ever recorded.[9]

Literary historians have taken this passage to anticipate the "rise of realism," which of course it does. But it is worth noting, in the context of my remarks here, that Whitman—like Emerson and others of their coevals—also referred to "nature" and its fatally polysemous cognates to justify their way with history both before the Civil War and after. As A. O. Lovejoy long ago tried to teach, to claim to do what comes naturally is to claim to justify the status quo—to say that what one is doing is what one must *perforce* do.

For the Whitman of the Civil War period, such doing increasingly ruled out a sense of obligation to the very pastness of the past, the fact of historicity, of proving personally the usual recorded, documentable facts of the past by silent meditation. A 17 January 1863 draft letter to Emerson (never sent) declares an intention to write "a little book out of this phase of America," which would once and for all indicate that here and now is all the evidence that one needs for our greatness.[10] A 19 March 1863 letter declares baldly:

These Hospitals, so different from all others—these thousands, and tens and twenties of thousands of American young men, badly wounded, all sorts of wounds, operated on, pallid with diarrhea, languishing, dying with fever, pneumonia, &c. open a new world somehow to me, giving closer insights, new things, exploring deeper mines than any yet, showing our humanity, (I sometimes put myself in fancy on the cot, with typhoid, or under the knife,) tried by terrible, fearfulest tests, probed deepest, the living soul's, the body's tragedies, bursting petty bonds of art. To these, what are your dramas and poems, even the oldest and tearfulest? Not old Greek mighty ones, where man contends with fate, (and always yields)—not Virgil showing Dante on and on among the agonized & damned, approach what here I see and take a part in. For here I see, not at intervals, but quite always, how certain, man, our American man—how he holds himself cool and unquestioned master above all pain and bloody mutilations. It is immense, the best thing of all, nourishes me of all men. This then,

9. Charles Godfrey Leland, *Sunshine in Thought*, ed. B. T. Spencer (1862; rpt. Gainesville, Fla.: Scholar's Facsimiles and Reprints, 1959), pp. 4-5.

10. *Collected Writings: Correspondence*, ed. Edwin Haviland Miller, 6 vols. (New York: New York University Press, 1961), 1:169 (all further citations to this work will appear in the text).

what frightened us all so long! Why is it put to flight with ignominy, a
mere stuffed scarecrow of the fields. O death where is thy sting? O
grave where is thy victory? &c. (pp. 81-82)

A 6 January 1865 letter announces that Whitman has ready a small
volume to be called *Drum-Taps*, which "has none of the perturbations of
Leaves of Grass": the poet is still satisfied with the latter but will make
some eliminations in the "next issue," having discovered in it "some
things . . . I should not put in if I were to write now" (p. 247). By
September 1866 a letter proclaims, "I assume that Poetry in America
needs to be entirely recreated" (p. 287). Mastering his terror of war and
death, then, the poet as American would discover and rediscover, in
sickness and in health, the present, and so would exorcise the past.
Whitman wrote in August 1866, when the 1867 edition was in press,
what apparently was intended to be but what was not used as the introduction:

> I claim that in literature, I have judged and felt every thing from an
> American point of view,—which is no local standard, for America to
> me, includes humanity & is the universal.
>
> America, (I have said to myself) demands one Song, at any rate, that is
> bold, modern and all-surrounding as she is herself. Its scope, like hers,
> must span the future & dwell on it as much as on the present or the
> past. Like her, it must extricate itself from the models of the past, and,
> while courteous to them must be sung from depth of its own native
> spirit exclusively.[11]

The poet of the future—who is the poet of the 1867 *Leaves of Grass*
and of the versions that follow—is so by virtue of being the poet of the
present, not the poet of the present as it derives from the past but the
present as it is extricable from the past. The deletion of those lines from
the 1860 version of "To a Historian" manifests the beginning of the
transformation of a poet for whom the problem of the past had become,
under whatever sociocultural and personal pressures (I do not know
enough to speculate on the latter), no problem because it was as problem nonexistent.

The quantum of genuine historical sensibility, a concern with the
historically registered past as it is in fact amenable to the registering, is, I
freely admit, quite modest. But it does quite crucially characterize the

---

11. *Walt Whitman's Blue Book*, 2:xiii.

1855 *Leaves of Grass*—quite crucially because most noticeably. It is, in the full context of the 1855 *Leaves of Grass* (and also in that of the 1860 *Leaves of Grass*, with its articulation according to the structure of what I have elsewhere called "archetypal autobiography"),[12] perhaps best understood as the deepest and fullest expression of Whitman's sense, in 1855, of temporality itself—a sense which, like the sense of history and historicity, pretty much survived through 1860, then rapidly and disastrously diminished.

Examples. First, in 1855, midway in the poem that came to be called "A Song for Occupations":

> Will the whole come back then?
> Can each see the signs of the best by a look into the
>   lookingglass? Is there nothing greater or more?
> Does all sit there with you and here with me?
>
> The old forever new things . . . . you foolish child!
>   . . . . the closest simplest things—this moment with
>   you,
> Your person and every particle that relates to your person.

1860: the passage remains pretty much the same. 1891-1892, via a series of revisions that begin in 1867:

> Will the whole come back then?
> Can each see signs of the best by a look into the looking-
>   glass? Is there nothing greater or more?
> Does all sit there with you, with the mystic unseen soul?
>
> Strange and hard that paradox true I give,
> Objects gross and the unseen soul are one.

In all versions, a shifting catalog of occupations is immediately set forth, but the adduction of "the mystic unseen soul" serves to transform passage through time to transcendence of time. The phrase "mystic unseen soul" is introduced in Whitman's annotations to his copy of the 1860 edition. The hard-edged catalog of occupations that follows in the 1860 edition is marked for striking out, so that an increasingly sentimentalized catalog is made way for. Historicity would

---

12. See my introduction to the facsimile 1860 *Leaves of Grass* (Ithaca: Cornell University Press, 1961), rpt. in *Historicism Once More* (Princeton: Princeton University Press, 1969), pp. 200-239.

appear to have been too demanding for the poet as his life moved from 1860 to 1867 and beyond.

Further examples: "Who Learns My Lesson Complete" (perforce I refer to the poems by the 1891-1892 titles) in its 1855 version centers on a series of flatly, temporally set autobiographical bits. Starting in 1867, they increasingly disappear; thus the poet's past, his altogether human past, disappears. Although the text of "There Was a Child Went Forth" appears to have been pretty much held to from 1855 to 1891-1892, it suffers subtle but absolutely basic changes as regards its dealing with temporality. The tense of the poem up to its concluding lines is the simple past ("*went* forth," and so on). In the 1855 and 1860 editions, we read at the end:

> These became part of that child who went forth every day,
>   and who now goes and will always go forth every day,
> And these become of him or her that peruses them now.

That last line, making understanding the past a necessary condition of understanding the present, is marked for deletion in Whitman's copy of the 1860 edition and is deleted in editions from 1867 on, so to achieve that separation of past and present prefigured in the massive changes in the specifically historical segments of the original—and originative— *Leaves of Grass*. In the 1855 "Song of the Answerer," there is a carefully managed shift of verbs from past to present tense. By 1891-1892 the shift, thus the understanding of temporality, has disappeared. Virtually everything is in the universal present, so that the poet is not historian but prophet. Finally, the most extreme example: "The Sleepers," is from the outset set in the present tense. In the 1855 version the poet insists, even though this version is set in the present, on the historicity (understood autobiographically) of his experience:

> O hotcheeked and blushing! O foolish hectic!
> O for pity's sake, no one must see me now! . . . . my
>   clothes were stolen while I was abed,
> Now I am thrust forth, where shall I run!
>
> Pier that I saw dimly last night when I looked from the
>   windows,
> Pier out from the main, let me catch myself with you and
>   stay . . . . I will not chafe you;
> I feel ashamed to go naked about the world,

And am curious to know where my feet stand . . . . and what
    is this flooding me, childhood or manhood . . . . and
    the hunger that crosses the bridge between.

The cloth laps a first sweet eating and drinking,
Laps life-swelling yolks . . . . laps care of rose-corn,
    milky and just ripened:
The white teeth stay, and the boss-tooth advances in
    darkness,
And liquor is spilled on lips and bosoms by touching
    glasses, and the best liquor afterward.

Whitman allowed the passage to stand through the 1867 edition but by
1891-1892 had deleted it, with its quite straightforward insistence on
conflating a sense of temporality with an altogether sexual sense—mas-
turbatory, homosexual, and heterosexual—of time-binding and -bind-
edness. These changes show that he would appear to have been
terrified—and who can *ex post facto* blame or gainsay him?—by his
explorations into the relationship between what it would still be well to
call personalism and historicism. (Perhaps one day psychoanalytic
understanding, transformed through amalgamation into a full philosophical anthropology, will at least let us imagine what was happening
to Whitman, even as we know it to be happening to ourselves.)

Whitman, I conclude, no more than his great peers could keep alive
that historical sensibility and its necessary component of historical actuality in a United States headed into and caught up in the Civil War—in
which, as in all genuinely revolutionary situations, a sense of history is
first quite physically reduced to a sense of contemporaneous survival and
then, by way of guilty rationalization, ideologized into a sense of a
utopian future. Whitman, always latently the prophet as opposed to
the historian, even the visionary, suffered toward what came naturally
and became the utopian of "Passage to India" in particular and the
1891-1892 *Leaves of Grass* in general. His master, Emerson, found himself forced to attack the very social consequences of the utopianism and
progressivism from the outset latent in his thinking. Thoreau, having
set forth his this-worldly utopian measure of man in *Walden* (1854), died
too young, frustrated in his attempt, after much research and some
thousands of pages of notes, to see how that measure would stand up
when put in the context of American Indian life, in which—so his
researches let him know—history and historicity, because the data were

not available, were not quite relevant. Hawthorne, at long last in the Custom House preface to *The Scarlet Letter* (1850) insisting that his tales of the past had always been tales for the present, thereafter tried repeatedly to write about contemporaneous life as it derived from life in the past and repeatedly found himself increasingly unsure of what he was about; at the very end he declared himself—and the sense of the past built into his sense of himself—overwhelmed by the present.[13] And Melville, toward the end of his career as a writer of fiction, first (in the latter part of *Israel Potter* [1855]) invoked a sense of the battle between the *Bon Homme Richard* and the *Serapis* as piercing as that invoked by Whitman in the 1855, 1856, and 1860 "Song of Myself." Only where Whitman had brought himself to live with the invocation by understanding it as an overmastering "fit," Melville transformed the episode into an appendage (or introduction) to a grotesque joke. (It is a nice fact for the historian that the first *Leaves of Grass*, thus the first "Song of Myself," and *Israel Potter* were both published in 1855.) Then Melville went on to *The Confidence-Man* (1857), in which he systematically, with an intense, almost suicidal satire, undercut the principal models of American self-trust and self-belief. The alternative to Whitman's millennialist utopianism after the 1860 *Leaves of Grass*, the alternative to his initial commitment to the glorious possibilities for the future that would issue from the American's "meditating silently alone" on his past, could only have been a Melvillian reduction of the American "personality" to that primitive state whence it would have once more to begin at the beginning. "Who's that describing the confidence-man?" Melville has his shape-shifting protagonist sleepily inquire at the time Whitman is projecting the 1860 *Leaves of Grass*. The point is, I take it, that by now we

---

13. Thus Hawthorne's dedication of *Our Old Home* (1863) to Franklin Pierce:

> I once hoped, indeed, that so slight a volume would not be all that I might write. These and other sketches, with which, in a somewhat rougher form than I have given them here, my Journal was copiously filled, were intended for the side-scenes, and backgrounds, and exterior adornment, of a work of fiction, of which the plan had imperfectly developed itself in my mind, and into which I ambitiously proposed to convey more of various modes of truth than I could have grasped by a direct effort. Of course, I should not mention this abortive project, only that it has been utterly thrown aside, and will never now be accomplished. The Present, the Immediate, the Actual, has proved too potent for me. [*The Centenary Edition of the Works of Nathaniel Hawthorne*, ed. William Charvat et al. (Columbus, Ohio: Ohio University Press, 1963), vol. 5, *Our Old Home*, p. 4.]

all, a writer named Herman Melville chief among us sinners, are on our way to being confidence men.

I daresay that in all cases—that of Emerson, Thoreau, Hawthorne, Melville, as well as of Whitman—there occurred a huge error, a huge failure of nerve. What with the Civil War and all that preceded it, I do not see how the error was avoidable. Yet I can imagine the error having been avoided. Accordingly, I think that we are caught in the position of relating that which was in utopian fact avoidable to that which was in non- (not anti-) utopian fact not avoidable: "there . . . the blow was struck, *for us*, as we ourselves in that place would have done or applauded." In short, reading and rereading the 1855 *Leaves of Grass*, I think it useless to chide Whitman for not having avoided the error, since it did occur and since American history as he and the others in signifi-cant part comprise it is in fact *our* history. That it is our history means that it is over but not done with. In the present, in the central paradox of the humanistic imagination, it can best be lived with when made subject to conditional-contrary-to-fact second-guessing—in medita-tions like this one, in which questioning history via the counterfactual is a necessary condition of entertaining it as an alternative to the fac-tual—that is, as a fiction, as poetry, as hope. Not in dreams but in history begins responsibility.

From this perspective, I would maintain that there *was* an error—however much, in documentable retrospect, unavoidable—and that "silently meditating alone" the work of Whitman and the others we might come to confront and know it as error. It is the error of *forget-ting*—as Whitman did when, revising the 1860 "To a Historian" for the 1867 *Leaves of Grass*, he dropped this line, ineluctably parenthetical as it is to our continuing sense of ourselves if we are in fact to continue:

> Let the future behold them all in me—Me, so puzzling and
> contradictory—Me, a Manhattanese, the most loving and
> arrogant of men;

In point of historical fact—when I am revising this meditation for I hope the last time—I have removed the parentheses from this line, thus creating the conditions of that counterfactual whereby we may, as the tried but true saw has it, let the poems read us—let both the successes and failures of the poems read us. Indeed, I hope that even as they are reading what I have written, some of those so occupied will have considered removing the parentheses too, thus as we all must, to recover *in* our history, and only *in* our history, ourselves not as we are driven to long for the primitive or utopianly millenarian but, as a wiser poet than Whitman put it, as we may bring ourselves to live *nel mezzo del camin*: however, as even that wiser poet would not have put it, *always* to live *nel mezzo del camin*—ever puzzling and contradictory, ever most loving and arrogant.

1981

7

"YOURS TRULY, HUCK FINN"

1

Huck Finn's closing words, as he is about to light out for the Territory, pose a dilemma not for him but for his reader.[1] Huck has been throughout a liar aspiring to be a shape-shifter, or vice versa. And he has not been altogether successful in either role. Moreover, as if his failure weren't enough, he is burdened—so one interpretive line has it[2]—with the failure of Mark Twain to invent for him in the final, the Evasion, chapters an action and a demeanor that will, from a reader's perspective, justify his special mode of credibility, his own way with the truth.

The problem centers on the ending of *Adventures of Huckleberry Finn*, to which in the end I shall come, in the hope of demonstrating that Huck has in fact, in the ironic rendering of his very factuality, wholly deserved that "Yours Truly," although at a great cost to us; and surely at a greater cost to Mark Twain. (Understanding this last would entail understanding the relationship between Samuel Clemens and Mark Twain—something beyond my competence.) For we must come to realize that rather than being possibly one of us—someone with whom, according to the canons of nineteenth-century realism, we might "identify"—Huck is exclusively a project of his own, Mark Twain-given possibility: in the end we must acknowledge the impossibility of

1. This essay is a conflation and development of two previously published: " 'The End. Yours Truly, Huck Finn': Postscript," *Modern Language Quarterly* 24 (1963):253-56; and "Huck Finn in His History," *Etudes Anglaises* 24 (1971):283-91. I am grateful to the editors of those journals for allowing me to reprint material they have published.

2. The major critique, of course, is Leo Marx, "Mr. Eliot, Mr. Trilling, and *Huckleberry Finn*," *American Scholar* 22 (1953):423-40.

his truth—all of it, and on its own terms—being ours. In the end we discover that we belong "realistically" at best with the Tom Sawyers of Huck's and our world, at worst with the Colonel Sherburns and the Dukes and the Dauphins—and, in a kind of merciful artistic transcendence, with the Mark Twains. But we also discover in the end that we are only possibly Tom Sawyers, Colonel Sherburns, Dukes and Dauphins, Mark Twains. Hope for something better, defined with high irony, does remain. But not for those interpreters among us who want guarantees beyond hope. The hope of *Huckleberry Finn* is the hope of utopianism, but necessarily (because ours is the way of the world of Tom Sawyer, of Colonel Sherburn and the Duke and the Dauphin, of Mark Twain) a failed utopianism. *Huckleberry Finn teaches* us (we should not flinch at the phrase) that whereas utopianism is possible, utopians are not.

Huckleberry Finn, then, is the sort of book that becomes absolutely central to the experience of a reader, American or otherwise, who would try to understand his sense of himself as against his sense of his culture. Its domain is Western America, but its purview, as in its art it universalizes Huck's experience, is the whole world. Through Huck's account of his world and those who inhabit it, Mark Twain renders Huck for us too—Huck at once in his world and apart from it. This of course is the abiding pattern of most of the masterworks of nineteenth-century American fiction, which project for our experience and understanding the central problem for the American in the nineteenth century, and also in the twentieth: How, in Emerson's words, satisfy the claims of the self as against those of the world? How, in Whitman's words, conceive of the person who must exist simply and separately and also as part of the mass? The major protagonists of nineteenth-century fiction before Mark Twain are put through trials and tribulations whereby they are readied for a return to a society whose integrity they, in seeking too fiercely to discover their own private identities, have somehow violated. At the end Hawthorne's Hester, Melville's Ishmael, and many others of their kind are ready to accommodate themselves to their society, and in their newfound knowledge of the complexities of relations between self and society are perhaps capable of contributing to the "improvement" of both. The tales told of them are open-ended, finally ambiguous and problematic. Under such terminal conditions, they have earned their right to try out the future. They have come to be endowed with a sense of their own history.

None of this is true of Huck. Return and accommodation—above all, the capacity to be an agent of "improvement"—are quite beyond him. His function, it turns out, is to demonstrate the absolute incompatibility of the sort of self he is and the sort of world in which he tries so hard to live. He gains no sense of his own history and has no future. Nor, as I shall show, need he have. Unlike Hester, Ishmael, and their kind, unlike the kind of committed person whom Emerson and Whitman envisaged, Huck neither could nor should be one of us. He exists not to judge his world but to furnish us the means of judging it—and also our world as it develops out of his.

The means to the judgment are the superb comedy and satire deriving from Huck's quite immediate and lyrical accounts of his own person and from his resolutely deadpan rendering of the doings of those among whom he has his adventures. The lyrical accounts abound and almost always establish his consonance with the natural world, as opposed to the civilized:

> Miss Watson she kept pecking at me, and it got tiresome and lonesome. By-and-by they fetched the niggers in and had prayers, and then everybody was off to bed. I went up to my room with a piece of candle and put it on the table. Then I set down in a chair by the window and tried to think of something cheerful, but it warn't no use. I felt so lonesome I most wished I was dead. The stars was shining, and the leaves rustled in the woods ever so mournful; and I heard an owl, away off, who-whooing about somebody that was dead, and a whippowill and a dog crying about somebody that was going to die; and the wind was trying to whisper something to me and I couldn't make out what it was, and so it made the cold shivers run over me.

Against this tone, there is that of the witness to civilized falseness, foolishness, and cruelty to others. Here, Huck and Jim have taken on the Duke and the Dauphin, and Huck has listened patiently to their outrageous stories about themselves:

> It didn't take me long to make up my mind that these liars warn't no kings nor dukes, at all, but just low-down humbugs and frauds. But I never said nothing, never let on; kept it to myself; it's the best way; then you don't have no quarrels, and don't get into no trouble. If they wanted us to call them kings and dukes, I hadn't no objections, 'long as it would keep peace in the family; and it warn't no use to tell Jim, so I didn't tell him. If I never learnt nothing else out of pap, I learnt that the

best was to get along with his kind of people is to let them have their own way.

The range in style—from lyrical to matter-of-fact—delineates Huck's character. In the latter style, he can make judgments, but no judgments that lead to significant action. Above all, he is not one to change the world. What is important is that he be allowed at critical moments to be himself, so as to combine in that self the directness, naiveté, and often helplessness of a boy with the practical wisdom of a man, clever in the ways of surviving in towns and woods and on the river. His authentic self as Mark Twain develops it makes him essentially a witness, even when he is a participant. His is a vital presence. In the long run, what he does is altogether secondary to what he is.

It was, as we now know, Mark Twain's original intention to involve Huck all the way in the practical—and in effect radical—action of helping Jim achieve his freedom. Hence the opening words of chapter 15 consolidate the action thus far: "We judged that three nights more would fetch us to Cairo, at the bottom of Illinois, where the Ohio River comes in, and that was what we was after. We would sell the raft and get on a steamboat and go way up the Ohio amongst the free States, and then be out of trouble." It is in this chapter, too, that Huck's instinctive sense of Jim as a person becomes clear; he can even bring himself to "humble [himself] to a nigger" and not be sorry for it. In the next chapter, although he is conscience-stricken at realizing what helping Jim means, still he protects him. And then they discover that they have gone by Cairo, are still on the Mississippi in slave territory. If Mark Twain had let Huck and Jim find Cairo and the Ohio River, he would have realized his original intention and made Huck into the moderately "activist" type he first conceived him to be. Likely the story would have ended there. In any case, Mark Twain knew little or nothing about the Ohio River and almost everything about the Mississippi and would have been hard put to find materials with which further to develop the story. In his plotting he seems to have come to an impasse. For he stopped writing at this point, in 1876, not finally to complete *Huckleberry Finn* until 1883.[3] At the end of chapter 16, a steamboat smashes the

---

3. See Henry Nash Smith, *Mark Twain: The Development of a Writer* (Cambridge: Harvard University Press, 1962), pp. 113-37, and Walter Blair, *Mark Twain and Huck Finn* (Berkeley: University of California Press, 1960), for basic accounts.

raft, and Huck and Jim, diving for their lives, are separated. In the context of the Evasion episode, the fact of Mark Twain's impasse is worth pointing out, because the Huck of the rest of the book, although continuous with the Huck of the first sixteen chapters, is not confined to his own small world and the river, not just dedicated (but in an agonized way) to helping Jim achieve his freedom, but also made witness to the full panoply of people and institutions that, as we see even if he does not, would deny freedom not only to Jim but also to themselves.

Between October 1879 and June 1883, while he finished *A Tramp Abroad* and *The Prince and the Pauper*, Mark Twain was able to write only chapters 17-21 of *Huckleberry Finn*; for he still had not discovered the means of turning Huck's adventures with Jim into something of a wider compass. During the winter of 1882-1883, he was writing *Life on the Mississippi*, developing it out of a series of magazine articles, "Old Times on the Mississippi," published in 1875. In preparation for that development he had revisited the Mississippi River and was depressed to see how much of all that he had so lovingly recalled in the magazine articles was disappearing. Indeed, his life during the period 1876-1883 had been difficult and too often personally disappointing. Traveling to Europe, he despaired of the development of those traditional free institutions that most of his contemporaries had persuaded themselves had been Europe's glorious gift to the world. Reading Dickens's *Tale of Two Cities*, Carlyle's *History of the French Revolution*, and Lecky's *History of European Morals*, he began to think of man's history as only confirming the view he (and his collaborator, Charles Dudley Warner) had taken of corruption in government and business in *The Gilded Age* (1873). Thinking about the Mississippi again, meditating the downward path from past to present, finding his increasingly desperate view of the human situation confirmed by his reading, he discovered his imagination empowered and vivified. It was as though he were compelled to finish *Huckleberry Finn*. He finished a draft of the book during the summer of 1883, spent seven months revising it, and saw it published in England in December 1884 and in the United States in February 1885.

Despair, then, is, as antecedent and consequence, a prime characteristic of *Huckleberry Finn*. But in the book itself it produces mainly comedy and satire of a superb order. For counterbalancing the despair that went into the writing of the book, there is the abounding joy of

Huck when he is most fully himself. In all his cleverness and dexterity, he is—except for what he does for Jim—essentially passive. He lives in the midst of violence and death; yet his only violence, if it can be called that, is the mild, ritualistic sort whereby when necessary he feeds himself. He hunts and fishes only when he has to. His joy is virtually private—to be shared, because instinctively understood, only by Jim. He is of course given no comic or satiric sense. He is given only his own rich sense of himself—richest when he is alone with Jim, on the river.

Comedy and satire derive from Huck's conviction that he must report fully what he sees—and further from the fact that it is he, capable of such joy, who does the reporting. Irony, a product of a tightly controlled point of view, is everywhere enforced for us by the fact that Huck, all unknowing, is its agent. He does not understand much of what he sees. Mark Twain's irony, however, lets us understand. What Huck is witness to again and again are doings of people who have contrived a world that distorts the public and private institutions—ranging from forms of government to forms of play—that just might make his sort of joy possible for all. His relationship with Jim—gained through his acceptance of the private guilt entailed by refusing to accept the injunction called for by public tradition and law—stands as a kind of utopian pattern for all human relationships. And we judge those in the book accordingly. Still, it is an appropriately primitive, even precivilized relationship; for Huck sees Jim not as a man with the responsibilities of a man but as one essentially like himself. This is his fundamental limitation, and yet the source of his strength. So long as that strength exists, so long as he exists, he can participate in the world only as a role-player, willing to go along with all the pretensions and make-believe that he witnesses. He accepts other names, other identities, almost casually. Living them, he seems to "belong" in his world. But not quite. For always there is a certain reserve. Always there is the joy of the simple, separate self, to which he returns again and again as though to renew himself. Set against that self, the world in which he has his adventures can be constituted only of grotesque, marvelously distorted beings who are the stuff of comedy and satire.

In 1885, planning to "get up an elaborate and formal lay sermon on morals and conduct of life, and things of that stately sort," Mark Twain defined Huck's situation in his world:

Next, I should exploit the proposition that in a crucial moral emergency a sound heart is a safer guide than an ill-trained conscience, I sh'd support this doctrine with a chapter from a book of mine where a sound heart and a deformed conscience come into collision and conscience suffers defeat. Two persons figure in this chapter: Jim, a middle-aged slave, and Huck Finn, a boy of 14, . . . bosom friends, drawn together by a community of misfortune. . . .

In those slave-holding days the whole community was agreed as to one thing—the awful sacredness of slave property. To help steal a horse or a cow was a low crime, but to help a hunted slave . . . or hesitate to promptly betray him to a slave-catcher when opportunity offered was a much baser crime, and carried with it a stain, a moral smirch which nothing could wipe away. That this sentiment should exist among slave-holders is comprehensible—there were good commercial reasons for it—but that it should exist and did exist among the paupers . . . and in a passionate and uncompromising form, is not in our remote day realizable. It seemed natural enough to me then; natural enough that Huck and his father the worthless loafer should feel and approve it, though it now seems absurd. It shows that that strange thing, the conscience—that unerring monitor—can be trained to approve any wild thing you *want* it to approve if you begin its education and stick to it.[4]

Not only the distinction between heart and conscience but also the quite sophisticated notion of how culture, or society, or the world, forms conscience and so makes possible the death of the heart—these conceptions are central to the very structure of *Huckleberry Finn* as Mark Twain finally developed it, as is the fact that he gives Huck a sense of his own heart which, at however great a cost, persuades him that he can be in the great world only a player of roles.

At the beginning Huck tells us that this time, unlike the occasion of *Tom Sawyer*, he is going to speak out on his own and so correct Mark Twain in a few matters. His truth, in a consummate irony, is to be set against the conscience of even his creator. Huck now is letting himself be civilized and reports mildly on how it is. Yet at the end of the first chapter (in the first passage cited above), we know that he is in full possession of his truthful self. Assured of that fact, we can rest easy

4. Quoted in Blair, *Mark Twain and Huck Finn*, pp. 143-44, copyright 1960 by the Mark Twain Co.

while he goes along with Tom Sawyer's complicated make-believe and even plays a trick on Jim. His sojourn in the Widow Douglas's world, as in Tom's, is throughout marked by role-playing and make-believe. And he can as easily adjust to his father's world, play his role there and sustain the make-believe, as he can to Tom's and the Widow Douglas's. Perhaps the patterns of make-believe in *their worlds* are harmless; no one is hurt much; everyone can make himself out to be aspiring to something better or nobler. But the pretenses and distortions of his father's world are dangerous and frightening; and Huck suffers accordingly— still managing, however, to record, in his frankness, his sense of his own truth. The make-believe and role-playing of Tom's boy's world are Huck's way into the make-believe and role-playing in the world of adults. The formal design is surely carefully contrived, allowing us easily to move with Huck from one world to the other, and demanding of Mark Twain that at the end of the adventures he arrange things so that Huck attempts to come back to his proper world, which, according to a proper pattern of conscience-directing institutions, must be a boy's world.

Indeed, the episodes of *Huckleberry Finn* evolve one into the other on Huck and Jim's trip downriver as so many exempla of the nineteenth-century American "conscience—that unerring monitor"—as it "can be trained to approve any wild thing you *want* it to approve if you begin its education early and stick to it." The murder of Pap, Jim's running away, Huck's information-seeking visit with Mrs. Loftus, their finding the wreck of the *Walter Scott*, Huck's cruel joke on Jim and the beginning of his sense of dedication and obligation to him, the separation, Huck amid the Grangerfords in all their distorted pride and nobility, his escape from the feud and reunion with Jim—these opening episodes, as we recall them, regularly involve Huck as either role-player or witness, or both. At their conclusion (at the end of chapter 18 and the beginning of chapter 19), Huck with Jim on his own, is his truest self:

> We said there warn't no home like a raft, after all. Other places do seem so cramped up and smothery, but a raft don't. You feel mighty free and easy and comfortable on a raft.

* * *

> Two or three days and nights went by; I reckon I might say they swum by, they slid along so quiet and smooth and lovely.

So it goes for the time being; and we are reassured. But almost immediately Huck and Jim are with the Duke and the Dauphin, consummate
artists in those forms of make-believe that fool all of the people most of
the time, possessors of consciences distorted enough to make them
(most of the time) masters of all whom they survey—including Huck
and Jim. Again (in the second passage cited above), Huck is willing to
go along. Or rather, he has no option but to go along.

The point is that he knows what he is doing, and accordingly we are
reassured that his sense of his authentic truth will sustain him. He
stands by—what else can he do?—while the Dauphin bilks a Pokeville
camp-meeting and the Duke takes over a print-shop and while they
fleece the public with their promised obscene "Royal Nonesuch" show.
Too, he is witness to Colonel Sherburn's denunciation of a small-town
mob and his shooting-down of the town drunkard. There is no impulse
to prevent any of this; this is beyond his capacities—after all, like the
rest of the townspeople he too is fooled by the act of the comic drunk in
the circus. Make-believe, all of it, and constant role-playing, but this
time his role is set according to his truth. The failure of this attempt of
the Duke and the Dauphin brings them to sell Jim. And there comes
Huck's great crisis, in which truth once and for all triumphs over conscience, instinct over training, the self over society and all the good and
needed things it offers.

The famous passage (in chapter 31) begins:

> Once I said to myself it would be a thousand times better for Jim to
> be a slave at home where his family was, as long as he'd *got* to be a slave,
> and so I'd better write a letter to Tom Sawyer and tell him to tell Miss
> Watson where he was. But I soon give up that notion, for two things:
> she'd be mad and disgusted at his rascality and ungratefulness for leav-
> ing her, and so she'd sell him straight down the river again; and if she
> didn't, everybody naturally despises an ungrateful nigger, and they'd
> make Jim feel it all the time, and so he'd feel ornery and disgraced. And
> then think of *me*! It would get all around, that Huck Finn helped a
> nigger to get his freedom; and if I was ever to see anybody from that
> town again, I'd be ready to get down and lick his boots for shame.
> That's just the way: a person does a low-down thing, and then he don't
> want to take no consequences of it. Thinks as long as he can hide it, it
> ain't no disgrace.

This is the voice of conscience, and it torments Huck. He tries to pray but realizes he "can't pray a lie." For he knows he will sin against his conscience by continuing to try to help Jim. He goes so far as to write a letter to Miss Watson, telling her where Jim is, and feels "all washed clear of sin." But then he recalls his relationship with Jim and makes the great decision—to "steal Jim out of slavery again." And so he says, "All right, then, I'll *go* to hell."

But stealing Jim out of slavery, it turns out, is yet a matter of role-playing. At the Phelpses, Huck is taken for Tom Sawyer and thereupon enters the last of his adventures—once more by assuming the name and, in part, the conscience of another. Tom comes, assumes his brother's name, and plunges them both into the work of the Evasion. Fittingly, necessarily, Huck must be brought back into that segment of the society that is, by the world's standards, appropriate to him—a boy's world.

The complications of the Evasion episode, and also its detail and length, tend to put off many readers of *Huckleberry Finn*. They see it as Mark Twain's evasion of the moral implications of his story, especially when they learn that Jim has been free all along. Huck, they say, should have seen Jim all the way to freedom. It might well be that the episode is in fact too complicated and too long, overbalancing the end of the story. Still, in the necessary scheme of the novel, in the necessary contrast between Huck's assumption of various forms of conscience and the truth he constantly has within him—in that scheme, it is imperative that the book begin as it ends: in effect, with a grotesque and sardonic comment on the nature of the forms of make-believe, pretense, and distortion that set the life-styles of those whose consciences they shape. It is all in the end very stupid. Men have given up the authentic truth they might well have had as children for the falsifying forms of con-science that lead to the violence, destruction, and predation that trans-form their society into the enemy of the very men it should sustain and preserve. Tom Sawyer here as before patterns his play principally after the romances of Sir Walter Scott. For boys it is moderately harmless play, although Tom is slightly wounded in the final scuffle. Yet we recall the episode of the wrecked steamboat, itself called *Walter Scott*, and are forced to realize what will necessarily ensue when boyish make-believe and role-playing become the mode of life of mature men and women. Conscience will not let truth survive.

Indeed, in this world Huckleberry Finn cannot continue to exist. He says at the end that he will not return to St. Petersburg: "I reckon I got to light out for the Territory ahead of the rest, because Aunt Sally she's going to adopt me and sivilize me and I can't stand it. I been there before." The plan to go to the Territory is Tom's, of course, for whom it is another opportunity for "howling adventures," this time "amongst the Injuns." Huck will survive, that is to say, by playing yet another role in this make-believe, conscience-stricken world. Here, however, he speaks only as witness.

2

In the last chapter of *Huckleberry Finn*, Huck in fact speaks twice of going to "the Territory." The first time he is reporting Tom's plans, now that the Evasion has been managed successfully, "to slide out of here, one of these nights, and get an outfit, and go for howling adventures amongst the Injuns, over in the Territory." The second time he is speaking of his own plans: "I reckon I got to light out for the Territory ahead of the rest, because Aunt Sally she's going to adopt me and sivilize me and I can't stand it. I been there before."

I suppose that the obvious irony of the two passages has not been pointed out precisely because it is so obvious. The Territory is, of course, the Indian Territory, which was to become Oklahoma. From the 1820s on, it had been organized and developed as a region to which Indians could be safely removed away from civilized society, since their lands were needed for higher purposes than those to which they could put them. The cruelty and deprivations of removal were generally taken to be the inevitable price American society had to pay as it passed through its God-ordained stages of development. One part of this price was said to be the yielding of a certain amount of freedom or, to put it as an article of faith in Manifest Destiny, the surrendering of a "lower" for a "higher" freedom.[5] It seems fairly evident that the man who was to write "To the Person Sitting in Darkness" and other such pieces would be fully aware of the removal episode, with its justifications and consequences, and that he intended his readers to be aware of it too. Read in this light, what for Tom is yet another willful adolescent fantasy becomes for Huck a compelling actuality. Tom's willfulness effects a parody that points up some of the grotesqueness of the historically

5. See my *Savages of America* (rev. ed., Baltimore: Johns Hopkins University Press, 1965), pp. 56-61.

authentic pioneering, civilizing spirit. Huck's compulsion effects a satire that simply denies that that spirit is authentic, despite its historical actuality. Huck will seek the freedom of the Territory just because it is an uncivilized freedom. (A better word, perhaps, is *noncivilized* freedom.) It is, indeed, the only true freedom for the authentic human being Huck eventually comes to be—in spite of himself.

Yet there is more to the passages, particularly the second, than this. Huck, we recall, speaks of lighting out for the Territory "ahead of the rest." Here, at the end, Mark Twain introduces his own point of view, which, of necessity, is more encompassing than Huck's; as a result Huck is given more to say than he could possibly know.[6] From Huck's simple point of view, the allusion is to Tom's vague plans to go to the Territory; for Mark Twain, it is to the Boomer movement that was a prime factor in the taking over of Indian lands, "sivilizing" the Territory, and creating another American state. The effect is that Huck, all unknowing, is given a kind of prescience that his adventures at this point surely justify. No matter where he goes, he will be one step ahead not only of the Tom Sawyers of his world but also of the sort of people into whom the Tom Sawyers grow.

After the Civil War, there was constant agitation in Kansas and Missouri to open up the unsettled parts of the Indian Territory to whites. To this end, bills were repeatedly, if on the whole unsuccessfully, introduced in Congress. Pressures were put on the so-called Five Civilized Nations (Cherokees, Creeks, and Choctaws principally) to cede part of their lands in the Territory to be used as reservations for other Indians and, for due payment, to make them available for settlement by whites. In the late 1870s and into the 1880s, white incursions into the Territory were numerous enough to call for the use of troops to defend Indian rights. Moreover, in 1879 a court decision found that even those lands in

6. Smith, *Mark Twain*, pp. 134-37, points out that the Colonel Sherburn episode derives from Mark Twain's point of view and thus is intrusive, a "flaw" in the structure of *Huckleberry Finn*. I think, however, that one must argue for Huck as a "reporter" and in this and other episodes (particularly that of the Evasion) wherein he is in no position to participate in, or at least dominate, the action and so render it in terms wholly congruent with his sensibility and understanding. The question is: How much irony are we to allow Mark Twain? An incidental burden of this interpretation is that in the end we must allow him enough and demand only of his novel that it "contain" its elements of irony.

the Territory that had been ceded to the government by Indians could not be settled by other Indians.

Inevitably, however, white incursions—by groups who came to be known as Boomers—increased in tempo and number. Invaders were not jailed but fined. When they could not pay the fines, they were simply escorted to the territorial border by soldiers. The economics of the situation were complex: railroads encouraged and propagandized Boomers; cattlemen, wanting to use the lands for grazing, opposed the Boomers, who were farmers, and defended the Indian rights, which included the right to rent their lands for grazing. The story (one of confusion, broken promises, and violence—all in the name of "civilization") moved toward its resolution in 1889, when the government bought certain lands from Indians and opened them to settlement as the Territory of Oklahoma.[7]

Boomerism, then, was the most recent expression of the westering American spirit. In the words of an 1885 petition to Congress, drawn up by B. L. Brush and John W. Marshall in Howard, Kansas, on behalf of Boomerism:

Resolved, That we are opposed to the policy of the Government in using the army to drive out or interfere with actual settlers upon any of the public domain, as being foreign to the genius of our institutions. . . .

Resolved, As this selfsame, bold spirit, that is now advancing to the front, has ever existed since the Pilgrim Fathers set their feet on Plymouth Rock, and will ever exist so long as we remain citizens of this grand Republic, that we, the citizens of Howard and vicinity, pledge ourselves to firmly support this grand element—the vanguard of civilization. . . .

Resolved, That we are opposed to the settlement of any more bands of wild Indians on the Indian Territory.[8]

Although I know of no direct allusion in Mark Twain's writings to the troubles in the Indian Territory, I think it likely that he was well

7. The story is best outlined in Roy Gittinger, *Formation of the State of Oklahoma, 1803-1906* (Norman: University of Oklahoma Press, 1939), pp. 68-157. On the Boomers, see Carl Coke Rister, *Land Hunger: David L. Payne and the Oklahoma Boomers* (Norman: University of Oklahoma Press, 1942).
8. Gittinger, *Oklahoma*, pp. 272-73.

aware of them, for they were widely publicized and debated and of great interest to Congress. A considerable amount of Boomer ferment developed in Mark Twain's—and Huck's—Missouri, although Kansas was a more important center. The summer of 1883, when Twain was writing the last part of *Huckleberry Finn*,[9] David Payne and his Boomers were particularly active in promoting their cause. One historian of Oklahoma reports that the general whose responsibility it was to turn Boomers back declared that in 1883 "the whole affair had become simply a series of processions to and from the Kansas line."[10]

Thus it would seem that in 1883, Mark Twain, now finally committed to a conception of Huck Finn whose fate it must always be to seek a freedom beyond the limits of any civilization, ended his novel by contrasting Tom's and Huck's sense of the Territory. Note that Huck is willing to go along with Tom, if he can get the money to outfit himself for those "howling adventures amongst the Injuns." Jim tells Huck that, now that his father is dead, he does have the money. However, he will have to claim it himself. The matter of the money and the "howling adventures" is then dropped. Since Tom is "most well" now, Huck says, there "ain't nothing more to write about." He will "light out for the Territory ahead of the rest." In one sense, perhaps, he simply means ahead of Tom and Jim; in a larger sense (so I think we must conclude) he means ahead of all those people whose civilizing mission Boomerism actualized in fact. The realities of the case are, as ever, contrasted with Tom's fantasies.

The Huck who seems willing to go along with Tom is, of course, not the Huck who, against the dictates of his conscience, has helped Jim in his quest for freedom. It is altogether necessary that this latter Huck must, alone, "light out for the Territory ahead of the rest." With the curious prescience that Mark Twain gives him, he knows that in antebellum days (as Mark Twain surely knew that summer of 1883), even in the Territory, he will be only one step ahead of the rest: Boomers, Dukes and Dauphins, Aunt Sallies, Colonel Sherburns, and Wilkses—civilizers all. Certainly we are not to assume that Huck self-consciously knows the full meaning (even the full moral meaning) of what he says here. Yet we cannot conclude that this allusion is simply a matter of

9. Walter Blair, "When Was *Huckleberry Finn* Written?" *American Literature* 30 (1958):1-25.
   10. Gittinger, *Oklahoma*, p. 131.

Mark Twain speaking out in his own person. Huck's view and Mark Twain's, in a culminating irony, here become one. Huck's prescience is, within the limits of the narrative, a matter of intuition, forced into expression by his hardheaded sense that he has almost always been one step "ahead of the rest." He can say his final "Yours Truly" and yet must be willing to go to hell for saying it.

3

I think we must conclude that Huck is not meant to survive. He is so powerfully a being of truth as against conscience, self as against society, that he exists not as an actuality but as a possibility. In him Mark Twain projects the American's sense that somewhere, at some point—even if only in the imagination—it would indeed be possible to regain access to the truth, if only we could cut through the shams of conscience and of the institutions that form and justify it. But in the present situation, Mark Twain despaired of that possibility and in Huck, his nature, and his history saw it only as impossible. Huck, then, is that ideal, perhaps never-to-be-attained type—in Wallace Stevens's phrase, an "impossible possible philosopher's man." Huck, then, stands as witness to his experience, totally unaware of the irony whereby it becomes at once an aspect and a function of our experience. In rendering the witnessing, Mark Twain makes us, if we but grasp the irony, the judge of that experience—Huck's and our own—and the world in which it is shaped. It is inappropriate to regret that Huck does not follow through on his own to free Jim. That is not Huck's proper role; for it would be the role of someone in whom conscience and truth were to a significant degree harmonious. Huck, for whom conscience always means role-playing, in whom the naked truth must finally be overpowering, stands, as I have said, not as possibly one of us but rather as our means of judging his world and Mark Twain's—and, along with it, ours.

We can take Mark Twain's preliminary "Notice" to *Huckleberry Finn* with the deadly serious levity with which it is meant: "Persons attempting to find a motive in the narrative will be prosecuted; persons attempting to find a moral in it will be banished; persons attempting to find a plot in it will be shot." "Motive" and "plot" are, however, not so much absent as negative. Huck's motive is to survive; and we know that the conditions of his life and of his society are such that survival is impossible. The plot of his *Adventures* lays out the pattern of the impossibility; Huck's is a history of whose meaning he cannot be conscious and still be his truest self. Above all, the story has no "moral." Rather it is an exercise in the use of such moral sensibility as remains with us. Knowing what Huck is, we can know what we have become and measure the cost and the worth.

F. Scott Fitzgerald wrote in 1935,

> Huckleberry Finn took the first journey *back*. He was the first to look *back* at the republic from the perspective of the west. His eyes were the first eyes that ever looked at us objectively that were not eyes from overseas. There were mountains at the frontier but he wanted more than mountains to look at with his restive eyes—he wanted to find out about men and how they lived together. And because he turned back we have him forever.[11]

The condition of his turning back, however, is that we cannot demand that he be one of us. He stands as witness, bound to his own truth, so that we might go forth and be likewise.

1985

---

11. I quote the statement from the original typescript, with the kind permission of its owner, Prof. Matthew Bruccoli. It has been previously printed in *Fitzgerald Newsletter* 8 (Winter 1960).

8

THE CRY AND THE OCCASION: REREADING STEVENS

1

To justify, so to explain, my title. First, the twelfth section of "An Ordinary Evening in New Haven":

> The poem is the cry of its occasion,
> Part of the res itself and not about it,
> The poet speaks the poem as it is,
>
> Not as it was: part of the reverberation
> Of a windy night as it is, when the marble statues
> Are like newspapers blown by the wind. He speaks
>
> By sight and insight as they are. There is no
> Tomorrow for him. The wind will have passed by,
> The statues will have gone back to be things about.
>
> The mobile and the immobile flickering
> In the area between is and was are leaves,
> Leaves burnished in autumnal burnished trees
>
> And leaves in whirlings in the gutters, whirlings
> Around and away, resembling the presence of thought,
> Resembling the presence of thoughts, as if,
>
> In the end, in the whole psychology, the self,
> The town, the weather, in a casual litter,
> Together, said words of the world are the life of the world.

Second, the seventh section of "Credences of Summer," one of Stevens's two favorite sections, so he wrote in a letter of 1953:

> Far in the woods they sang their unreal songs,
> Secure. It was difficult to sing in face

Of the object. The singers had to avert themselves
Or else avert the object. Deep in the woods
They sang of summer in the common fields.

They sang desiring an object that was near,
In the face of which desire no longer moved,
Nor made of itself that which it could not find . . .
Three times the concentred self takes hold, three times
The thrice concentred self, having possessed

The object, grips it in savage scrutiny,
Once to make captive, once to subjugate
Or yield to subjugation, once to proclaim
The meaning of the capture, this hard prize,
Fully made, fully apparent, fully found.

We are instructed in the first passage that the poem inseparably derives from its occasion—the poem is the cry not "on" its occasion but "of" its occasion, generated by it. We are instructed in the second passage that the making of the poem, if it would not avert itself from its object, is a three-stage affair, in effect a dialectical process. Now, the second passage dates from 1950 and the first from 1949, so that, properly interpreted, they themselves project, over time, a dialectical process: from defining and delimiting the poem to acknowledging and elucidating the process of its composition. What I want to suggest here is that the dialectic entailed is also that of reading the poem—which is a matter of *rereading* the poem. And rereading means not just reading again and again, repetitively, but reading in three distinctly and progressively different modes. Capture is a mode of possession. Subjugation and yielding to subjugation are modes of identification. Meaning can be proclaimed only as the result of this process carried all the way through—"fully," as Stevens most explicitly says. Thus the poem as in the end, worked through, the cry of its occasion. The object, first possessed, then identified with, has been discovered as an occasion. For the reader this means that somehow, then, he must determine the nature of the occasion, not for its own sake but rather for the sake of understanding the cry that celebrates it and, so celebrating, celebrates itself. The pun res/race is of course fundamental, as it declares that the things *of* this world are altogether human things.

Ironically—and Stevens was an ironist quite beyond the ken of his New Critical contemporaries—one identifies (or emphathizes) with the occasion so as in the end to be released from it, released through it. (Res becomes race becomes res. . . .) But the mode of release—its very substance and style, its dialectic—is initiated and therefore in significant measure controlled by the occasion. Psychologically and epistemologically the situation is that of the double bind, as though the poet were saying to us: Remember to forget this. A problem for us, to be sure. In the long, the longest, run, a problem—*the* problem—for the poet too. For in the context of poetic fictions—as opposed to that of life through lived day-to-day—the situation of the double bind produces in the person whose bind it is (if the fictions work) an increased and increasing tolerance for those ambiguities that appear to be central to the human situation.

I suggest, then, that the three-stage dialectic of writing and reading can be classified—to use terms of which Stevens was fond, terms on which Stevens depended—as Invention, Decreation, and Re-creation. Rereading Stevens—reading Stevens fully—then is a matter of with him working through this dialectic.

Invention is at once discovery and creation, a mode of reading that entails exegesis, explication, exploration, puzzling out, above all attending most closely to details, so as to interrelate and integrate them. It is a mode quite adequate to reading, say, Eliot and Pound, since it is the mode whereby their poems were composed, whereby they are integrated toward a *terminus ad quem*. It continues, perhaps necessarily, to be the dominant mode of reading in Anglo-American criticism at least (even in 1986!) and remains an absolutely necessary condition of successfully moving to Decreation and Re-creation.

A recent graceful summation of the inventive mode is this, all the more significant because it occurs in a book that, concerned with what the author perceives to be the deterioration of late modernist (thus "post-modernist") literature, finds Stevens (along with Henry Miller!) to preadumbrate that deterioration:

> All through the modernist era, literature, like disciplined thought and art in general, continued to be energized by a shared confidence in the writer's fundamental power over everything contingent. It was a power to transcend confusion; to bring equilibrium out of conflict; to reconcile those contradictions which are paralyzing or worse; to restore balance, remedy deprivation, reverse entropy, substitute protocols of concord and relation for evolutionary turbulence; to give freely, and

sympathize, and control; to demonstrate the immediate sensible reality of love and freedom or their terrible opposites; and in all these ways to suggest a human figure still conceived as potentially open and reparative.[1]

This is to call in theme and form for a stasis and certitude which entail that sense of an ending ranging from proclaiming that we must give, sympathize, and control, to exclaiming Yes, Yes, Yes, to triumphantly resigning ourselves to meditating casual flocks of pigeons as they sink downward to darkness on extended wings.

Most reading of Stevens, that is to say, has taken the mode of "Sunday Morning" and related poems, the inventive mode, as its paradigm. For we have been instructed how to read Stevens not by him but by the more-or-less formalist (call it middle I. A. Richards) tradition in which many of us have been raised and have taught and written and whose components I have just listed. I fully grant that much of the most powerful and effective reading of Stevens has been in the mode of Invention. But that fact has meant that the most powerful Inventors, if I may call them that, somehow have found that the later poems—for which the exercise of the inventive mode alone simply is not adequate—are not as satisfactory as the earlier and middle poems, for which the inventive mode alone almost—I emphasize *almost*—suffices. Thus, for example, one of the most effective of the Inventors, Randall Jarrell, in 1951 found the *Auroras of Autumn* collection altogether inadequate as poetry. Yet in 1955, reading the *Rock* sequence, he could write, "As we read the poems we are so continually aware of Stevens observing, meditating, creating, that we feel like saying that the process of creating the poem is the poem."[2] Jarrell, I suggest, like others of the powerful Inventors, was not quite ready to read (to read and reread in the terms I have outlined) the *Rock* sequence; yet—and this is what is important—he was seeking a way to ready himself. He could have found it had he noted that Stevens in "An Ordinary Evening in New Haven," collected in *The Auroras of Autumn*, had in Section XXII substituted for the word *create* the word *re-create*:

> Creation is not renewed by images
> Of lone wanderers. To re-create, to use

1. Warner Berthoff, *A Literature without Qualities* (Berkeley: University of California Press, 1979), p. 102.
2. "The Collected Poems of Wallace Stevens," *Yale Review* 44 (1955):346.

> The cold and earliness and bright origin
> Is to search. Likewise to say of the evening star,
> The most ancient light in the most ancient sky,
>
> That it is wholly an inner light, that it shines
> From the sleepy bosom of the real, re-creates,
> Searches a possible for its possibleness.

The way *toward* Re-creation, the way toward being able to say of the evening star that, in spite of its ancientness, it is wholly an inner light, is the way of Decreation, as Stevens, adapting a by now celebrated passage from Simone Weil, came to call it. The passage is in the 1951 essay "The Relations between Poetry and Painting":

> decreation is making pass from the created to the uncreated, but . . . destruction is making pass from the created to nothingness. Modern reality is a reality of decreation, in which our revelations are not the revelations of belief, but the precious portents of our own powers. The greatest truth we could hope to discover, in whatever field we discovered it, is that man's truth is the final resolution of everything.[3]

(Recall that in "The Man with the Blue Guitar" Stevens speaks of Picasso's painting, which he did not like, as a "hoard / Of destructions," in fact echoing Picasso's description of his own art as a "sum of destructions.") For Stevens, then, it is "man's truth," known as "the precious portents of our own powers," whereby, through Re-creation, we may search out "a possible for its possibleness." But as a necessary condition of that search we must acknowledge that our reality—even the reality of the evening star—whatever it has been in the past, whatever its origins and previous significations, now, in the present, is *for us* "uncreated," simply given, not informed by any extra-human power or system, not at all mythic, not at all carrying a guaranteed component of intrinsic meaningfulness. Yet we must remember (or learn in order to remember) the nature of that distinctively past meaningfulness—this as a necessary condition of the decreative mode, whereby (the double bind) we may forget, or almost forget, what we have remembered, perforce have struggled to remember.

A poem in the decreative/re-creative mode, then, is necessarily somewhat different in form and function from a poem in the inventive mode.

3. *The Necessary Angel: Essays on Reality and the Imagination* (New York: Knopf, 1951), pp. 174-75.

It is open-ended, frankly speculative and ratiocinative, its structural integrity and unity deriving from the occasion that, decreated, gives it its originating impetus—its continuing impetus deriving from the re-creative powers of the poet. That we have not yet learned to acknowl-edge these conditions is demonstrated by this quite recent comment by a pair of critics, M. L. Rosenthal and Sally M. Gall, who must be cautionary when they are about to discuss Stevens's "Auroras of Autumn" as a principal exemplar of that "Modern Poetic Sequence" which they find to be "The Genius of Modern Poetry." They write:

> As we have noted, the speculative, ratiocinative mode invites the dan-ger of shifting away from presentation and sliding into sheer dis-course. . . . A consistent voice, a rational argument, the logical exploration of related themes, can provide a surface that not only con-ceals a work's lyrical structure (the relation of its crucially decisive units of affect) but smothers it to death. Frequently, too, even with the rela-tively independent poems or sections, the . . . sequence sustains a cer-tain formal consistency that militates against the wide shifts of tone and texture natural to the sequence. These problems occur in even so fine a work as Stevens's "The Auroras of Autumn."[4]

I suggest that we might well decreate this passage, as I have tried to do by echoing its language, so as to make it an initiating occasion for consideration of Stevens's achievement in the re-creative mode.

Stevens in any case came to know exactly what he was doing. A pre-1951 anticipation of the need for the decreative mode—and accord-ingly of the re-creative mode—is developed in "Of Modern Poetry" (1940):

> The poem of the mind in the act of finding
> What will suffice. It has not always had
> To find: the scene was set; it repeated what
> Was in the script.
>   Then the theatre was changed
> To something else. Its past was a souvenir.

Some ten years after the publication of "Of Modern Poetry" came the texts and doctrines I have been discussing. According to these doc-trines, even as the poem is the cry of its occasion, the occasion itself must be decreated, must be—for modern man—taken as uncreated. Its

4. *The Modern Poetic Sequence* (New York: Oxford University Press, 1983), p. 361.

component of createdness must be acknowledged, so as to be subject to Decreation. And this then would precisely give rise to the need for Re-creation, a mode in which the evening star, that "most ancient light," could be decreated, then re-created as "wholly an inner light." First an acknowledgment (not quite an acceptance) of history and historicity; then—*force majeure*—an acceptance (not quite an acknowledgment) of history and historicity: in short, an expression of the obligation to de-historicize, which is of course much more profound than the impulse toward what is now fashionably called de-mythologizing.

Properly to read Stevens, then, we are confronted by a need to dis-cover occasions for the cries that are the poems, yet to discover those occasions as "uncreated"—that is, guided by the poet, to decreate them.

This fact, I think, demands, if we are to move beyond the mode of Invention, that we reconsider the relations of Stevens to his "sources," that we refine and redefine our notion of the role of "allusion" in his poems, that we take "sources," "allusions," and the like as "occa-sions"—aspects of a reality to be decreated, but to be decreated in order to make possible Re-creation. For Stevens the occasions are not produc-tive of fragments he can or would shore against his ruins, such frag-ments being not only contributive to but in good part constitutive of the meaning and import of the poems in which they occur. We must, that is to say, undertake to discover the "occasions," with Stevens decre-ate them, and then with him re-create them in poems, always searching out a possible for it possibleness, which is a manifestation of our very own possibleness, an expression of Stevens's commitment to an ultimate and radical humanism. We shall, I think, realize that the occasions—if we but search them out—are precisely enough set forth to be delimit-ing, so that we shall find that Decreation is not at all deconstruction.[5]

5. The matter of decreation versus deconstruction is discussed in my "Toward Decreation: Stevens and the 'Theory of Poetry,'" *Wallace Stevens: A Celebration*, ed. F. Doggett and R. Buttel (Princeton: Princeton University Press, 1980), pp. 286-307. The essays in that volume by J. Hillis Miller (pp. 274-85) and by Joseph N. Riddel (pp. 308-38) succinctly set forth the deconstructionist view. I should note too that my own view of decreation in Stevens here differs from that I set forth in my *Continuity of American Poetry* (Princeton: Princeton University Press, 3d ff. printing, 1965), pp. 412-13. The growth, as I like to think of it, in my understanding of Stevens and decreation is owing to severe application of the historicist mode in interpretation. For alternative historicist views of Stevens, see, for example, Frank Lentricchia, *After the New Criticism* (Chicago: University of Chicago Press, 1980), and Fredric Jameson, "Wallace Stevens," *New Orleans Review* 11 (1984):10-19. Even as I think deconstruc-

For Decreation—in preparing us for Re-creation—defines as much as it frees, confines as much as it releases, demands as much as it gives, questions as much as it answers.

2

Some examples, then. The first two show Stevens early on moving toward the decreative/re-creative mode. The others exemplify the mode as fully achieved.

i

Illustrated here is the simplest of occasions—an object that Stevens made into an occasion.[6] This of course is the occasion of "Anecdote of the Jar," first published in 1919. It is an ordinary fruit jar, widely distributed in the United States, so that Stevens could have seen one such when he was traveling in Tennessee April and May 1918. It is notable among fruit jars, for being a "wide mouth special" (recall that Stevens's jar is "tall and of a port in air"). And it is, compared to other fruit jars, especially "gray and bare." That is, the glass is more heavily leaded than is customary in fruit jars. Decreating his encounter with the jar in Tennessee, Stevens re-creates the occasion, so as to discover once more the precious portents—and inevitably the limitations—of his own powers. The poet, figuring himself as having composed a Tennessee landscape by the act of placing a fruit jar "upon a hill," comes to understand the expense of his act. It is the realization that out there, outside the scope of the "imagination" (to use one of Stevens's compulsively favorite terms), there is, there perdures, a "reality" (to use another), in its rudimentary existence totally beyond being conceived directly by him who would know it. Thus the double negative in the last two lines, which in effect discover that "everything" in Tennessee except the poet in the exercise of his imagination "give[s] of bird or bush"—of "reality."

That my sense of the occasion is correct has been recently demon-

tionist interpretation of Stevens's work misconstrues it, I think that my fellow neo-historicists err in their compulsion to find a "plot" as opposed to a "meaning" in the history that is around and in Stevens's poems.

6. I set forth here the matter of my " 'Anecdote of the Jar': An Iconological Note," *Wallace Stevens Journal* I (1977):64-65. I have adduced the information sent to me by Glenn McCleod in a private communication. The photograph of this jar, an exemplar I have in my possession, is by David Crowne.

The "Dominion Wide-Mouth Special" Fruit Jar

strated by Glenn McCleod in a study of Stevens's relations with his
Harvard College classmate Walter Arensberg and, through Arensberg,
with Marcel Duchamp, whose work Stevens often saw in Arensberg's
salon during the years around World War I. Duchamp invented what he
called the "readymade," placing an ordinary urinal on its side, for
example, calling it "The Fountain," and signing it "R. Mutt." A col-
league explained Duchamp's intentions which, however playfully,
anticipate Stevens's later accounts of the decreative/re-creative process:

> Whether M. Mutt with his own hands made the fountain or not has no
> importance. He CHOSE it. He took an ordinary article out of life,
> placed it so that its useful significance disappeared under the new title
> and point of view—created as new thought for that object.

The poem in the re-creative mode might at its most reductive simply be
defined as a new thought deriving from the poet's choice to bring about
the disappearance of the useful significance of objects he knows and the
occasion of the knowing, in order to manifest himself as poet—*poet*
being, as Stevens later said, a word for "any man of imagination."

ii

Another more or less iconological note, with again an illustration.[7]
By now we all surely accept R. P. Blackmur's brilliant explication of
"The Emperor of Ice Cream," which he summed up by writing, "The
poem might be called Directions for a Funeral, with Two Epitaphs."
Yet we are tempted to assume that the substance of the poem is rather
illusive than allusive. I think, as the illustration shows, that the poem is,
in Stevens's special sense, occasional, and that the occasion has been
decreated and then re-created, so that, double bind or no, we are miss-
ing something if we don't understand the occasion—not illusion but
rather allusion. Who is being addressed in "The Emperor of Ice
Cream"? Why and to what end "roller of big cigars," "The muscular

7. See my " 'The Emperor of Ice Cream': A Note on the Occasion," *Wallace
Stevens Journal* 3 (1979):53-55. The Ybor City historian whom I quote is Tony Pizzo,
"The Italian Heritage in Tampa," *The Sunland Tribune: Journal of the Tampa Historical
Society* 3 (1977):27. The photograph is reproduced courtesy of Ybor Square, Tampa,
Florida. It is of the V. M. Ybor Factory, which had been built in 1886. Although the
photograph dates 1925, it would appear that it fairly represents the state of such a
factory when Stevens would have seen it.

Tampa, Florida, Cigar Factory

onc," "Let the lamp affix its beam"? Why and to what end, above all, "ice cream"?

Stevens was in Tampa, Florida, so unpublished letters show, Thursday and Friday 15 and 16 November 1917. The Friday letter, written in the evening to his wife, reports the overpowering beauty of the flowers he has seen and also, without details, a couple of walks, the second around the town. Given his intensity as a walker in cities, Stevens seems—granting the opening lines of "The Emperor of Ice Cream"— to have walked to Ybor City, the cigar-manufacturing section of Tampa, which was (and is) within a mile or so of his hotel.

He could have looked at the sort of scene set in the photograph here given. By 1917 Tampa's Ybor City had become the great center for the manufacture of cigars of high quality. The cigar rollers were Cubans, Spanish, and Sicilian émigrés who had together created a genuine community. The photograph—and there are others that indicate this in more detail—shows men with muscular forearms (a product of their occupation) working together under well-placed lamps. Above them, in a kind of pulpit, is the "lector," who is reading in Spanish to them

from fiction, poetry, drama, and the newspapers—so to make their ten-
hour day not entirely a thing without joy. Their routine was eased too
by numerous coffee breaks; they were allowed all the free cigars they
wanted. And Stevens could have seen more of Ybor City, its clubs and
its coffeehouses—its notably *gemeinschaftlich* mien. There was something special about the coffeehouses. For the Sicilians coming to the
community in the 1890s had brought with them their cuisine and had
introduced it to the community, even as they had adopted the community's language. Ybor City's historian notes, "The Cubans who are
great lovers of *cafe solo* began enjoying the new pleasures of Sicilian
gelatti, such as granita or lemon sherbet and even more exotic ice creams
with the flavors of mulberry, prickley-pear, jasmine, cinnamon,
almonds, and watermelon." Readers of Stevens's correspondence,
recalling his compulsive search for flavors, will surely say Q.E.D.

Thus the occasion of "The Emperor of Ice Cream": a "lector"
addressed in such a way and in such a situation as to remind him of his
obligations as regards "Directions for a Funeral," to the end that the
poet—through Decreation and Re-creation—might earn the right to
his "Two Epitaphs" and his discovery once more that even while death
concludes (brings to a close) life, life can end (terminate) death. Out of
an occasion a transformation so complete as to make us wonder that it
was not a creation *ab origine*. But it is not. And that is the sticking
point, the telling point, the interpretive point.

The poem, then, surely is the cry of its occasion, all the more telling
for being so. The poem was first published in 1922.

iii

With "Chocorua to Its Neighbor" (1933), we may ourselves invent
the decreative/re-creative mode of those middle and late poems in
which it is paramount. Here, to give a full example of the matter of the
need to re-read Stevens, we must—if only to indicate the complications
of the matter—in our investigations go all-out. The rest might well
follow.

a

Mount Chocorua figures first in Stevens's poetry in the twenty-first
section of "'The Man with the Blue Guitar." Here the mountain represents the poet's capacity to discover the very potency of "reality," even
though the poem, as vehicle of discovery, is necessarily abstracted out of

and accordingly to be distinguished from reality, "things as they are."
This Chocorua thus is an early adumbration of the Supreme Fiction:

> This self, not that gold self aloft,
>
> Alone, one's shadow magnified,
> Lord of the body, looking down,
>
> As now and called most high,
> The shadow of Chocorua
>
> In an immenser heaven, aloft,
> Alone, lord of the land and lord
>
> Of the men that live in the land, high lord.

The shadow of the human, of the imagination, is projected so that it
becomes the shadow of the mountain, thus lordly even while inevitably
abstracted and separated from "one's land, / Without shadows, without magnificence, / The flesh, the bone, the direct, the stone."

The twenty-second section of "The Man with the Blue Guitar" is a
commentary on what has been figured in the twenty-first:

> Poetry is the subject of the poem,
> From this the poem issues and
>
> To this returns, Between the two,
> Between issue and return, there is
>
> An absence in reality,
> Things as they are. Or so we say.
>
> But are these separate?

And the twenty-third section, returning to the Chocorua motif (it can
be called, as I shall call it, a topos), projects the image of Chocorua and
its shadow as suggesting "a few final solutions" (the year was 1937, so
that the use of the phrase is coincidental yet minatory):

> . . . like a duet
> With the undertaker: a voice in the clouds,
>
> Another on earth, the one a voice
> Of ether, the other smelling of drink,
>
> The voice of ether prevailing, the swell
> Of the undertaker's song in the snow
>
> Apostrophizing wreaths, the voice

In the clouds serene and final, next

The grunted breath serene and final,
The imagined and the real, thought

And the truth, Dichtung und Wahrheit, all
Confusion solved, as in a refrain

One keeps on playing year by year,
Concerning the nature of things as they are.

All this—in particular the sense of the imagination as part of reality, a product of that reality which in modern times it is condemned in its acts to distort—points back toward the central theme of the poem, announced quite flatly in the fifth section, as Stevens insists on correcting Picasso, with the latter's too imperious sense of the artist's, thus the imagination's, powers:

Poetry

Exceeding music must take the place
Of empty heaven and its hymns,

Ourselves in poetry must take their place,
Even in the chattering of your guitar.

What is at issue are both the rewards and the costs, the losses, accruing from the act of the poem, which is for Stevens of course the act of the mind, the act of the imagination. This is the issue, what issues from, "Chocorua to Its Neighbor."

In "The Man with the Blue Guitar" such matters, as my quotations indicate, are treated as questions more to be at once puzzled, even celebrated, than resolved. In effect the poems collected in the volume of that name (1937) and in *Ideas of Order* and *Owl's Clover*, which immediately preceded it (1935, 1936), derive the questions they treat from the sorts of situations, predicaments, and encounters informing and setting the occasions for the poems of the *Harmonium* period (1923-1931). *Transport to Summer* (1947) contains the poems in which Stevens begins to design that dialectic entailed by his need to create, and understand in the creating, only in the creating, "the poem of the act of the mind." The principal poems in this mode, "Notes toward a Supreme Fiction" and "Esthetique du Mal," were of course first collected in *Transport to Summer*. So was "Chocorua to Its Neighbor," which had been first published in 1943. "Chocorua to Its Neighbor" at once recalls the twenty-first section of "The Man with the Blue Guitar," reinforces, by employing, the dialectical mode of "Notes toward a Supreme Fiction" and "Esthetique du Mal," and points all the way to the triumphant "Rock" sequence in *The Collected Poems* (1954). The "Rock" sequence is triumphant because the poems in it achieve the hard-earned wisdom of old age; the dialectic is for a time stabilized, and the poet can now imagine what it would be like to be transcending without being transcendent, a condition that we can see *ex post facto* has been his aspiration from the outset. The poet who had been driven to conceive his "hero," his "central man," as an "impossible, possible philosophers' man" can now envisage individual and individualized heroes, himself among them. My concern here is in general to show how all this is in greatest particular anticipated in "Chocorua to Its Neighbor," to show how that poem culminates a Chocorua topos and a Chocorua iconography in American culture, and to demonstrate that, receiving topos and iconography via Henry James's *American Scene* (1907), Stevens at the end of the poem in fact discovers—and decreates and re-creates—James as one of his heroes. What is at issue indeed is how and to what end "the poem is the cry of its occasion." The decreative/re-creative mode is now fully achieved.

b

"Chocorua to Its Neighbor" moves in three phases. The first, sections I through X, develops in the dialectical mode of "Notes toward a Supreme Fiction" to full conception of the "abstract" hero. The second, sections X-XII, is in the decreative mode and reveals, if only for an instant, the hero-in-himself before he was a hero, immanent in "reality." The third, sections XIII-XXVI, quite concretely and singularly achieves the re-creative mode: what Stevens had called for in the sixth section of the "It Must Be Abstract" segment of "Notes toward a Supreme Fiction": "An abstraction blooded, as a man by thought." The abstraction of the first phase of "Chocorua to Its Neighbor" is blooded by the decreative thought of the second phase, and the hero—who is Henry James—comes forth as an altogether human re-creation:

> How singular he was as man, how large,
> If nothing more than that, for the moment, large
> In my presence, the companion of presences
> Greater than mine, of his demanding, head
> And, of human realizings, rugged roy. . . .   (XXVI)

All is cast in the past tense. The "poem of the act of the mind," however, is such as to require of us that we read it as an act of the historical present—decreation become re-creation.

At the outset the mountain speaks of itself as involved in a universe so huge and large, so vastly general, as to be compelled to perceive "men without reference to their form." Quantities so large and so varied can be conceived, if the human is to conceive them at all, as qualities— necessarily abstracted qualities. Even the mountain, when the light of a morning star makes it possible, can conceive of itself only as a "prodigious shadow." (This is the "shadow magnified" of the Chocorua passage in "The Man with the Blue Guitar.") Abstracted as shadow, the mountain can conceive of its possibility as figuring the heroic—the past, in all its heroics, become the present:

> The feeling of him was the feel of day,
> And of a day as yet unseen, in which
> To see was to be. He was the figure in
> A poem for Liadoff, the self of selves:
> To think of him destroyed the body's form.   (IV)

The rest of this phase of the poem is given over to a series of exhaustingly paradoxical statements—self-transcending because self-negating, a fusion of extreme perceptions "which the eye / Accepted yet which nothing understood . . ." (VI). The mountain, abstracting shadow from what is shadowed, heroic from mundane self, third from first person, rests—but unsatisfied—in the paradox of the Supreme Fiction:

> Upon my top he breathed the pointed dark.
> He was not man yet he was nothing else.
> If in the mind, he vanished, taking there
> The mind's own limits, like a tragic thing
> Without existence, existing everywhere.   (VIII)

In the second phase, daylight comes, and the shadow-become-hero-become-third-person speaks. His speaking is a result, as I have said of this phase, of what Stevens came to call "decreation"—"modern reality" (the "things as they are" of "The Man with the Blue Guitar"), which results from "making pass from the created to the uncreated." As a mediating step in the imagination's movement from conception to inception, from discovery to recovery, from invention-as-finding to invention-as-making, decreation allows us at once to glimpse and to grant the existence of a world, and those—including ourselves—who inhabit it, over which, because of its sheer givenness, we have no control. It is that step in the imagination's movement at which, as Stevens later put it in "The Plain Sense of Things" (1952), "the absence of the imagination had / Itself to be imagined." Imagined thus, the newfound hero, as it were, de-abstracts himself, acknowledges his lonely particularity, and warns against that "enlargement" which will eventually be, however necessary it is in the search for a Supreme Fiction, grandiose and aggrandizing. He declares, "Of what I am, / The cry is part" (X-XI). Then:

> ". . . and the sound
> Of what is secret becomes, for me, a voice
> That is my own voice speaking in my ear.
>
> There lies the misery, the coldest coil
> That grips the centre, the actual bite, that life
> Itself is like a poverty in the space of life,
> So that the flapping of wind around me here
> Is something in tatters I cannot hold." (XI-XII)

Thus in the first two phases of the poem the hero as abstracted into a Supreme Fiction—therefore "not man"—and also the hero as decreated, therefore "nothing else." (One recalls "The Snow Man," with its final insistence on "nothing that is not there and the nothing that is"—a discovery that very early, 1921, entails the decreative mode.) In the third phase of "Chocorua to Its Neighbor," Stevens can go beyond the limits of "Notes toward a Supreme Fiction" and "Esthetique du Mal" precisely as he can go beyond demonstrating and celebrating attributes in discovering that being, quite concrete and particular, whose attributes they are. "He," heretofore an abstraction, comes alive. Again, speaking in its own person about its projection—now at once universal and concrete, abstracted and decreated—the mountain knows that it must live with and within a mystery. For decreation as a mode is but negative capability, a mode suited to a world whose reality Stevens elsewhere declares is constituted by "myth," now transformed dialectically into a negating capability, a mode, of course, suited to a world—a "modern" world—whose reality is in fact constituted by the absence of the myth-making imagination.[8] Having listened to its third-person shadowed

8. See, for example, letters of 10 December 1935 and 3 June 1953, *Letters of Wallace Stevens*, ed. H. Stevens (New York: Knopf, 1966), pp. 300-778.

projection, the mountain declares:

> In spite of this, the gigantic bulk of him
> Grew strong, as if doubt never touched his heart.
> Of what was this the force? From what desire
> And from what thinking did his radiance come?
> In what new spirit had his body birth?   (XIII)

Now the mountain understands and is sure. The mountain remains "it." But its "prodigious shadow" is "he," and, working through decreation, in him the mountain has achieved the singularly, the particularly, human. He—this abstraction blooded by decreative thought— "was more than an external majesty" (XIV). However heroic he might have been, he had to be of men, yet "excluding by his largeness their defaults" (XV). And, secure in its knowledge that he existed, "The collective being knew / There were others like him safely under roof" (XVI): a captain, a cardinal, a statue, a mother, a scholar—now, in this third phase of the poem, "True transfigurers fetched out of the human mountain" (XVIII). There comes a moment of high triumph. The poet is no longer one who sounds a barbaric yawp. But surely his is the same order of triumph—only now, and necessarily, adapted to a world whose reality is constituted by decreation, not by myth:

> To say more than human things with human voice,
> That cannot be; to say human things with more
> Than human voice, that, also, cannot be;
> To speak humanly from the height or from the depth
> Of human things, that is the acutest speech.   (XIX)

Now, as if to look back, so to discover how far it has come and what it has found, the mountain declares that it rejoices in its limitations— with its sense of this "shadow" as after all a "human thing," which will come and go and yet perdure; a human thing that is not an overwhelming father figure but brother, at once large and equal (in the nonce word "megalfrere"); a "common self"; at home resting on the very mountain whose originality of being it projects, not something distant and separate (XX-XXIII). "It," projected through its humanization, has indeed become "he." He lives entirely in this world (XXIII). He is "captain and philosopher," he is our small fortress, always there, though difficult at times to find (XXIV). Always he has searched "for what / Was native to him in that height, searching, / The pleasure of his spirit in the cold" (XXV). In his search, which is his art, he has endured, so that we might endure with him. He has become a particular and individuated man—from mountain to man to men and back, but now to "a" man. Again the conclusion:

> How singular he was as man, how large
> If nothing more than that, for the moment, large
> In my presence, the companion of presences
> Greater than mine, of his demanding, head
> And, of human realizings, rugged roy . . .   (XXVI)

A hero, a hero among heroes, yet in his history ineluctably one of us—living, having lived, and to live, on our behalf.

c

It seems most unlikely that Stevens knew Mount Chocorua at first hand. Although answering Renato Poggioli's June 1953 query about the twenty-first section of "The Man with the Blue Guitar," he wrote simply, "Chocorua is a mountain in New Hampshire," in June 1939 he had written to Henry Church, advising him with some enthusiasm to tour the White Mountains "in order to understand New England."[9] Yet, even though unpublished letters might make the matter clearer, Stevens's sense of Mount Chocorua would appear to be distinctly a literary sense, deriving immediately from Henry James's meditations on the mountain in *The American Scene* (1907) and proximately (perhaps through James) from a distinct inconography and topos.

The inconography can be dealt with quite simply and, in the context of this interpretation, shown to be but contributory to the topos involved. Mount Chocorua, as an exemplar of what Stevens wryly called the "American Sublime" in 1935, figures prominently in nineteenth-century New England landscape painting.[10] What is compulsively depicted is the stately, self-contained loneliness of the peak, often emphasized by contrasting it with the picturesque scene below, including Lake Chocorua. Indeed many of the paintings are virtually copybook exercises in deploying the models of the sublime versus picturesque. All this is conventional enough, and not altogether unex-

9. Ibid., pp. 783, 338
10. For details, see "The Cry and the Occasion: 'Chocorua to Its Neighbor,'" *Southern Review* 15 (1979):784. The Aaron Draper Shattuck painting is reproduced courtesy of the Vassar College Art Museum.

Aaron Draper Shattuck, Chocura Lake and Mountain

pected. Perhaps less expected—certainly most relevant to Stevens's poems—is the fact that regularly a mysterious looking cloud formation is depicted, often in the shape of the peak itself, as though it were Stevens's "prodigious shadow." Since, as we shall see, the matter of the "prodigious shadow" figures as a prominent element in the Chocorua topos (James's version of it included), the matter is at least worth remarking in passing. And the matter is all the more interesting in the context of Stevens's poem and the traditions that it culminates when one considers the fact that the director of Parks and Recreation for New Hampshire has written me, "Any reference in some of the older White Mountain books to the . . . 'shadow' of the mountain would be strictly historical in context since there is no present day reference to the above."[11] Stevens's context, then, is nothing if not historical: topographic in the etymological sense of the word.

   The Chocorua topos is set by two themes—that of the Indian Chocorua, his fate, and his curse, and that of the sublime/picturesque qualities of the mountain itself. The first is a minor theme, even as it is developed in Stevens's poem as the mountain is made to speak. The legend has it that Chocorua (the person) was driven to "curse" those who would come after him. James summarizes the legend as one "immediately local, of the Indian who, having a hundred years ago murdered a husbandman, was pursued by roused avengers, to the topmost peak of Chocorua Mountain, and thence, to escape, took his leap

11. George T. Hamilton to RHP, 28 July 1977.

into the abyss.["12] He does not mention the "curse"—Chocorua's proclamation that his was itself an act of revenge for a son accidently killed while being left in the care of white settlers—but would nevertheless appear to have had the entire legend in mind. As we shall see, James does have the mountain speak. And the speech is a blessing, or expression of a hope, rather than a curse. This transformation, decreation/re-creation, is what we have in Stevens's poem.

The sublime/picturesque aspect of the topos appears more insistently and is, of course, more important in an interpretation of Stevens—and also of James. Thus the following:

John Greenleaf Whittier in 1868:

> And once again Chocorua's horn
> Of shadow pierced the water.

Lucy Larcom in 1875:

> Hoary Chocorua guards his mystery well:
> He pushes back his fellows, lest they hear
> The haunting secret he apart must tell
> To his lone self, in the sky-silence clear.
> A shadowy, cloud-cloaked wraith, with shoulders bowed,
> He steals, conspicuous, from the mountain-crowd.

Julia Noyes Stickney in 1884:

> Scatter the haze and let me see
> Thy form, Chocorua, ere I go:

> Fair Juno's veil had hid from me
> A mountain shrine, that painters know,
> Above the blue-lake's flow.

John Albee, in 1892, meditating in a prose-poem on Chocorua's witnessing the division of man against woman below, after it had looked down upon the world "with sympathy":

> But never again did Chocorua take any pleasures in the affairs of man
> and woman. It withdrew; it raised itself once more to its ancient

12. W. H. Auden, ed., *The American Scene* (New York: Scribners, 1946), p. 15. Bibliographical data on the Chocorua topos are set forth in my "The Cry and the Occasion," p. 785.

heights, its primeval thoughts. And this is why, disappointed with mankind, it is to-day so haughty, so mysterious and incommunicable.

Frank Bolles in 1895:

> . . . All his [the bluejay's/man's] beauty is delusion,
> All his tricks are tricks of darkness;
> Grim Chocorua through his cloud veil
> Ever looks askance upon him.

Edwin Osgood Grover in 1895:

> Through the wide hush of heavens soft sunlit blue,
>   A universal prophet of the hills,
>   You cry: "The world grows old!" High in the stills
> And calms of lofty solitude I view
> The glory of the hoary head and through
>   The mellow misty shrine that floods and fills
>   The interspace thy ancient grandeur thrills
>   Adown the valleys, palpitant and new
>   Oh, patriarch of the hills!

And C. E. Whiton Stone in 1908:

> Heavy across thine unbared forehead lies
> The lifeless air, and stars that o'er thee shine
> Are dim with haze, that blurs the horizon lines
> Like smoke of unchecked fire: —Upon the skies
> The full moon swoons, and every leaf and vine
> Upon thine unstirred heart, seems worn as a sign
> Death has o'ertaken thee in sleep's disguise?—
> Inscrutable thou liest wrapt in light;
> And while the pines like tapers lit, I see
> Shine on, unflickering through the breathless night
> Beside thy massive couch, it seems to me
> Who see beyond, how measureless the white
> Earth, too, is dead, and lying in state with thee.

This vision of Chocorua—of the mountain and its "neighbor"—was summed up by Thomas Starr King in 1849. He wrote of "the two Chocoruas": "One is a rocky, desolate craggy-peaked substance, crouching in shape not unlike a monstrous walrus . . . ; the other is the wraith of the proud and lonely shape above."

It seems unlikely that Stevens would have known any of these pieces.[13] Henry James might well have known some of them, although one cannot tell from the published record. He did know Mount Chocorua at first hand, however, having visited his brother and family at their beloved summer retreat there in the fall of 1904.[14] Out of the visit—perhaps out of ancillary reading—came the Chocorua meditations in *The American Scene*, which were the occasion of "Chocorua to Its Neighbor." In *The American Scene* the Chocorua topos becomes history: transformed, decreated, it is to become the occasion of Stevens's poem. James, so characteristically at this stage of life, will see the individual in the general:

> Written over the great New Hampshire region at least, and stamped in particular, is the shadow of the admirable high-perched cone of Chocorua, which rears itself, all granite. . . . It had to pass for the historic background, that traceable truth that a stout human experiment had been tried, had broken down. One was in the presence, everywhere, of the refusal to consent to history.

This comes midway in James's account and is followed by his imagining the mountain to have been speaking:

> The touching appeal of nature, as I have called it therefore, the "Do something kind for me," is not so much a "Live upon me and thrive by me" as a "Live *with* me, somehow, and let us make out together what we may do for each other. . . . See how 'sympathetic' I am," the still voice seemed everywhere to proceed, "and how I am therefore better than my fate; see how I lend myself to poetry and sociability—positively to aesthetic use, give me that consolation."

The mountain, James variously insists, hopes for "the aesthetic enrichment of the summer people, so far as they should be capable or worthy of it, by contact with the consoling background, so full of charming secrets, and the forces thus conjoined for the production and the imposition of forms." These last words come at almost the very end of James's Chocorua meditation and sum up his sense that the mountain, the place, the scene, have been instructing the summer people that they had in fact better learn to consent to history and the time-locked and place-

13. See "The Cry and the Occasion," p. 787.
14. "My brother Henry stayed a delightful fortnight, and seemed to enjoy nature here intensely—found so much *sentiment* and feminine delicacy in it all. It is a pleasure to be with anyone who takes in things through the eyes. Most people don't." *Letters*, ed. Henry James (Boston: Houghton Mifflin, 1920), p. 215.

centered "forms" and "appearances" it manifests, precisely as the mountain, the place, the scene project the danger, the temptation, of the "complete abolition of forms." James moves toward his conclusion as regards the "aesthetic enrichment of the summer people."

> He [James himself] could make the absence of forms responsible, and he could thus react without bitterness—react absolutely with pity; he could judge without cruelty and condemn without despair; he could think of the case as perfectly definite and say to himself that, could forms only be, as a recognized accessory to manners, introduced and developed, the ugliness [of the "complete abolition of forms"] might begin scarcely to know itself. He could play with the fancy that the people might at last grow fairly to like them.[15]

To summarize and quote thus is, if that is possible, to reduce James's meditation to an argument, so the better to see in it the central occasion of "Chocorua to Its Neighbor." And there are of course verbal echoes, but put into forms of the double bind: for James's reiterated concern for "forms," Stevens's likewise explicitly reiterated concern; for James's sense, seeing the mountain, of "the poetry in solution in the air," the mountain's sense that its shadow has "breathed in crystal-pointed change the whole / Experience of night"; for James's emphasis on the evening star as interfusing the scene, Stevens's emphasis on the role of "the crystal-pointed star of morning"; for James's realization that here he was in danger of being overwhelmed by "naturalism in quantity," "quantity inordinate," Stevens's view of the whole world of reality as manifesting "a swarming of number over number"; for James's brief glance at the Indian standing at the top of the mountain, Stevens's note of Chocorua projected into a hero as having "more than muscular shoulders, arms and chest."

The decreated verbal echoes, however telling, are secondary to Stevens's development of James's argument. Still, they do serve to help identify James as the decreated hero of the third, re-creative phase of "Chocorua to Its Neighbor." For even as in the third person James as "he" comes to dominate his *American Scene* meditation, Stevens discovers for us increasingly as his poem moves toward its end the power of a hero singular enough to be named not "it" but "he." "It" is the stuff of a Supreme Fiction, which partakes of "myth." "He" is the stuff of

15. *The American Scene*, pp. 21, 25, 26.

history, myth, and the abstraction of the Supreme Fiction, once discovered for what they are and then decreated. Indeed, discovery and decreation together constitute the mode of James's meditation, in which he alternately allows himself to be forced into the celebrative and then probes for the particulars that, antecedent to the generalization, have been compounded into it. That is, it is overwhelmingly James's meditation, decreated, which in fact allows Stevens to move to the third, the re-creative, recovering phase of his poem, to blood his abstraction not only with his own but with what he discovers as James's decreative thought. James's most succinct definition of reality, one recalls, indeed implies the decreative process: "The real represents to my perception the things we cannot possibly not know, sooner or later, in one way or another; it being but one of the accidents of our hampered state, and one of the incidents of their quantity and number, that particular instances have not yet come our way."[16]

No book by James survives in what can be identified as Stevens's library. No matter, for at the very least Stevens's exegete must avoid that curious scholarly fallacy which assumes that one reads only the books one owns (or, for that matter, assumes that one has read all the books that one owns). More important, Stevens did quote from James in a letter of 20 June 1945, to José Rodriguez Feo—the quotation coming from F. O. Matthiessen's *Henry James: The Major Phase*. And he commented on the passage in a letter of 17 October 1945, to Feo: "A world of creation is one of the areas, and only one, of the world of thought and there is no passion like the passion of thinking which grows stronger as one grows older."[17] And in the key essay (key, we recall, because it expounds the idea of "decreation"), "The Relations between Poetry and Painting," he quoted from a James letter to H. G. Wells: "It is art which makes life, makes interest, makes importance . . . and I know of no substitute whatever for the force and beauty of the process"—this either directly from the Lubbock edition of James's *Letters* or from an as yet unidentified mediating source.[18] The affinities in the work of Stevens and James are, however, self-evident—so much, it seems to me, as

16. Preface to *The American*, New York Edition (New York: Scribners, 1907), 2:xv-xvi.
17. *Letters*, pp. 506, 512.
18. *Letters* (New York: Scribners, 1920), 2:490. The mediating source could have been *The Portable Henry James*, ed. M. D. Zabel (New York: Viking, 1951), in which James's letter to Wells is printed, pp. 487-89.

in the end to have made my exercise in occasion-hunting an exercise in
pietas. Stevens, as is well known, was fond of working from the older
to the newer meaning of "invention"—discovering as against creating.
This exercise has reversed the process: from being obliged to create an
occasion for (so the better to understand the argument of) "Chocorua
to Its Neighbor" to discovering the occasion as decreated and re-created
(so to identify its decreated hero, its singular, albeit re-created, man).
Inventing thus, one concludes that Stevens's conclusion is as inevitable
as necessary:

> How singular he was as man, how large,
> If nothing more than that, for the moment, large
> In my presence, the companion of presences
> Greater than mine, of his demanding, head
> And, of human realizings, rugged roy . . .

Toward the end of his life, Stevens wrote a number of retrospective
poems, interpretations and assessments of his work and life as poet. One
of these, first published in *The Collected Poems* in 1954, is "The Poem
That Took the Place of a Mountain":

> There it was, word for word,
> The poem that took the place of a mountain.
>
> He breathed its oxygen,
> Even when the book lay turned in the dust of his table.
>
> It reminded him how he had needed
> A place to go to in his own direction,
>
> How he had recomposed his pines,
> Shifted the rocks and picked his way among clouds,
>
> For the outlook that would be right,
> Where he would be complete in an unexplained completion:
>
> The exact rock where his inexactnesses
> Would discover, at last, the view toward which they had edged,
>
> Where he could lie and, gazing down at the sea,
> Recognize his unique and solitary home.

Here Stevens, resting satisfied ("complete") in dissatisfaction
("unexplained completion"), can at long last admit, therefore claim,
that, like James's, his has been by virtue of sharing in and contributing

to the collectively heroic, a singularly heroic existence. Thus "Chocorua to Its Neighbor" (to recall my opening quotation), compounded of cry and occasion, integral to the res/race, in the end yields a poet—one of us, yet that particular one in whose will, because it manifests ours, lies whatever peace we may have—re-creation made possible by decreation, reading made possible by re-reading.

iv

With "The Auroras of Autumn" (1948), we come to the highest decreative/re-creative mode, Stevens in a virtually chthonic mood. Decreation begins to move *adust*. For what is decreated at the outset is the serpent of universal creation myth, the serpent—head swallowing tail, wholeness guaranteed—as he is said to manifest the very continuity of existence and also to negate it. In both his functions he is present at the outset in the aurora borealis, that autumnal phenomenon whose very coloration and frequent ourobic form belie the beginning and end of seasonal bareness below; for there is only endless continuity. Indeed, Stevens's description of the serpent is, through his description of coloration and ouroborism, at the outset a setting forth of the decreative process:

> This is form gulping after formlessness,
> Skin flashing to wished-for disappearances
> And the serpent body flashing without the skin.
>
> This is the height emerging and its base . . .
> These lights may finally attain a pole
> In the midmost midnight and find the serpent there,
>
> In another nest, the master of the maze
> Of body and air and forms and images,
> Relentlessly in possession of happiness.
>
> This is his poison: that we should disbelieve
> Even that. His meditations in the ferns,
> When he moved so slightly to make sure of sun,
>
> Made us no less as sure. We saw in his head,
> Black beaded on the rock, the flecked animal,
> The moving grass, the Indian in his glade.   (I)

Thus what is involved is decreating the idea of decreation itself: the serpent's supreme poison. Successively Stevens in all decreative honesty details the sort of disbeliefs (so much more powerful than unbeliefs, because rejected, not ejected) that derive from modern man's incapacity to find an authoritative ground for belief in his origin, continuity, and end. The idea of place, of the familial, of a father-figure, of a mother-figure, of art, of imagination—none can be sustained. So that the idea of innocence, even the innocence of man's possible beginning, itself is lost, except as a "pure principle" which in all its purity is by decreative definition (by now become fiat) unattainable. Yet in all this, because innocence can be abstracted from experience as an ultimate possibility, *the* ultimate possibility, something is in fact gained, re-created: the precious portents of our own powers. Thus:

> This is nothing until in a single man contained,
> Nothing until this named thing nameless is
> And is destroyed.   (VI)

This dialectically earned conclusion is reached repeatedly, to culminate in the triumphant final (tenth) section:

> An unhappy people in a happy world—
> Read, rabbi, the phases of this difference.
> An unhappy people in an unhappy world—
>
> Here are too many mirrors for misery.
> A happy people in an unhappy world—
> It cannot be. There's nothing there to roll
>
> On the expressive tongue, the finding fang.
> A happy people in a happy world—
> Buffo! A ball, an opera, a bar.
>
> Turn back to where we were when we began:
> An unhappy people in a happy world.
> Now, solemnize the secretive syllables.
>
> Read to the congregation, for today
> And for tomorrow, this extremity,
> This contrivance of the spectre of the spheres,
>
> Contriving balance to contrive the whole,
> The vital, the never-failing genius,
> Fulfilling his meditations, great and small.
>
> In these unhappy he meditates a whole,
> The full of fortune and the full of fate,

As if he lived all lives, that he might know,

In hall harridan, not hushful paradise,
To a haggling of wind and weather, by these lights
Like a blaze of summer straw, in winter's nick.

This is to describe at the end the working of that ultimate poet, capable of sustaining the three-part dialectic (Invention, Decreation, and Re-creation) because capable of sustaining himself and the precious portents of his own powers. Not the fall of man. Rather the "full" of man: "The full of fortune and the full of fate. . . ." Which in penultimate fact derives from what Stevens had long before decided to call the imagination—but now understood as at once "the expressive tongue [and] the finding fang"—that is to say, to follow Stevens at the outset of "The Auroras," that which derives from the inevitable fact of the confrontation of creation and decreation: the latter figured as the "poison" in our ourobic skies.

v

"As You Leave the Room," written in 1955, the year of Stevens's death, not published until 1957, in *Opus Posthumous*, is doubly decreative, as it were. It in fact decreates an earlier poem, "First Warmth," written in 1947 but never published. And in and of itself it is in the decreative/re-creative mode. Because it is not well known, it must be quoted in full:

You speak. You say: Today's character is not
A skeleton out of its cabinet. Nor am I.

The poem about the pineapple, the one
About the mind that is never satisfied,

The one about the credible hero, the one
About summer, are not what skeletons think about.

I wonder, have I lived a skeleton's life,
As a disbeliever in reality,

A countryman of all the bones in the world?
Now, here, the snow I had forgotten becomes

Part of a major reality, part of
An appreciation of reality

And thus an elevation, as if I left

With something I could touch, touch every way.

And yet nothing has been changed except what is
Unreal, as if nothing had been changed at all.

Now the poet can look at his own work, take it as uncreated, simply given, and see fully how, even as it sums up a grand argument for the division between mind and reality, self and the other, it manifests the poet's central involvement in both. Stevens refers in turn to "Someone Puts a Pineapple Together" (itself a decreation of the Cubist aesthetic, 1947), where he had seen it as the poet's categorical imperative "to defy / The metaphor that murders metaphor," this phrase itself recalling the anti-Picasso sentiments of "The Man with the Blue Guitar"; to "The Well Dressed Man with a Beard"; to "Asides on the Oboe," "Examination of the Hero in a Time of War," and other related poems; and to "Credences of Summer," whose central passage I quoted toward the beginning of this interpretation.

"As you Leave the Room" is in effect a decreative survey of Stevens's poetry during precisely that period when he began to push it into its most "philosophical" mode. It was in this period, we should recall, that he had begun to try to solve the problems of belief and commitment raised so variously and movingly in "The Snow Man" (also referred to in "As You Leave the Room"), "Sunday Morning," "A High-Toned Old Christian Woman," "Le Monocle de Mon Oncle," and the rest— poems of high Invention all. (Although "The Snow Man" can be taken as a prescription for the decreative mode.) The "philosophical" poems—centrally "Notes toward a Supreme Fiction" and "Esthetique du Mal"—discover that the resolution of those problems is the fact that they are irresolvable, a discovery that commits the poet to that powerful humanism which, as we can see *ex post facto*, entails the decreative/re-creative mode. Now, in a poem that constitutes a kind of magisterial afterthought, Stevens can, by decreating his own work, thus his very self, discover that he has been at the center of things all along—as poet, not a divided but a whole man: or at least one capable of continually imagining himself to be whole, thus making himself whole. The glance all the way back to "The Snow Man" (1921) makes "As You Leave the Room" an exercise in retrospect become an exercise in redefinition: Decreation become Re-creation.

3

Thus five examples of the decreative/re-creative mode. There are many others that I am sure, had we world enough and time, could be spelled out. "The Comedian as the Letter C" in good part derives from a decreation of "The Waste Land." "The Well Dressed Man with a Beard" derives in good part from a decreation of *Sartor Resartus.* (It might well be called "Sartor Resartus Resartus.") "The Man with the Blue Guitar" derives in good part from a decreation of the work of Picasso, which Stevens, in that poem, as I have pointed out, called a "hoard / Of destructions." "An Ordinary Evening in New Haven" derives in good part from a decreation of the Book of Revelation, Stevens putting himself on the side of Ecclesiastes. "Of Mere Being" derives in good part from a decreation of the myth of the palm (that "palm at the end [not the beginning] of the mind") as the Tree of Life, so that in Stevens's beginning is his end. And so on. . . . In the light of this evidence, I feel that in particular we must reconsider Stevens's relation with a number of writers, translating the idea of allusion as influence to allusion as occasion: Laforgue, Mallarmé, Pater, Schopenhauer, Shelley, Keats, Nietzsche, Ramon Fernández, Charles Maurron, Santayana, Coleridge, Bergson, William James, and so many others. And we must search out other occasions. We must imagine these occasions as "uncreated"—for us as for Stevens, simply given, whatever their possible origins and original meanings, so that with Stevens we can move on in our reading to the mode of Re-creation. But there will always be that double bind: Remember to forget this.

Reading Stevens according to his dialectic—that of Invention, Decreation, and Re-creation—we shall better read all his poems. But of course we shall in particular better read the later poems, in which as I have said the dialectic is most fully manifest— "The Rock," to set a final example. In the realm of myth, history, and religion, the Rock itself is St. Peter's and all that St. Peter's signifies. But not in the realm of "modern reality." Decreated, it is the "ground" on and out of which with Stevens we might re-create ourselves, so to search for what he came to term the "ultimate" possible for its possibleness. The language of the poem is that of Christian dogma in particular and religion in general, decreated, so to be re-created:

> It is not enough to cover the rock with leaves.
> We must be cured by it as by a cure of the ground
> Or a cure of ourselves, that is equal to a cure
>
> Of the ground, a cure beyond forgetfulness.
> And yet the leaves, if they broke into bud,
> It they broke into bloom, if they bore fruit,
>
> And if we ate the incipient colorings
> Of their fresh culls might be a cure of the ground.
> The fiction of the leaves is the icon
>
> Of the poem, the figuration of blessedness,
> And the icon is the man.

Man is icon, *the* icon, because the rock of his existence has been invented, decreated, and re-created. (Only thus can we discover that "man's truth is the final resolution of everything.") The dialectic of the composition of the poem is also that of Decreation and Re-creation. In the first section of the poem, the poet decreates himself in the seventy years of his existence, only to rediscover and reaffirm his perduring capacity again to create, thus to re-create. In the second section (from which I have quoted), the poet creates by re-creating a new mode of sacramentalism, one for which he, as human, is totally responsible. And in the third section, he affirms that re-creating humanism:

> It is the rock where tranquil must adduce
> Its tranquil self, the main of things, the mind,
>
> The starting point of the human and the end.

The dialectic of the composition of the poem is also the dialectic of its reading. And that, I submit, is the dialect of rereading, thus in the end of once more inventing—because the dialectic is continuing—the union of the cry and the occasion.

4

Finally we must assess the costs as well as the rewards to Stevens of his three-part dialectic. The rewards are I hope by now self-evident: an ultimately humanistic poetry, even if its humanism is that of most modernist writers, the humanism of the one as opposed to the humanism of the many. Because it is in fact a humanism of the one—the fullest devel-

opment of what a while back I termed the Adamic mode, the antino-
mian mode, in American poetry (thus in American culture)—in the
end, because it is carried unflinchingly all the way, it has necessarily to
be an isolating humanism. Tradition, myth, orthodox religion—none
can be authoritative for Stevens as he discovers himself as modern man.
But he goes—he went—a step further. Even history, historicity, the
facts of the historical case, when decreated, appear to have for him been
such as to move him toward his self-imposed, because self-discovered,
isolation. And I write as one of those who aspires toward the humanism
of the many, as well as the humanism of the one—each both a necessary
and sufficient condition of the other. Thus I must be bold enough, even
as I am profoundly grateful for poems that taught me how to think,
how to read, to find them, however perfected in their intensity, to be
lacking in scope and compass and altogether human complication. For I
am impelled by the very power of Stevens's dialectic to declare that if
what can be decreated are the postulates and precipitates of the self in its
history (from God as a postulate of the ego to a mere fruit jar as one of
its precipitates), what cannot be decreated is the fact, the factuality, of
the self in its history—that is, historicity as such. For the burden of
historicity as such, along with the burden of its twin, ambiguity (we
recall the entailment of the double bind by the decreative mode), is a
necessary condition of that very human situation which at once defines
and enables the very possibility of humanity, *humanitas*, itself. Withal,
precisely ("particularly") because of what is necessitated by this declaration, I have nonetheless found myself bound to discover that Stevens's
poems were made "particularly" for me. Inasmuch—*De mortuis nihil
nisi verum*—as they were made for me, I must declare them to be lacking, as the culture—my culture—whose idea, modes, and styles fueled
them is lacking.

Apparently Stevens found his poems lacking too. At least, that is one
way of understanding his apparent death-bed conversion to Roman
Catholicism, which might well have been a desperate measure toward
re-creating the Palm at the expense of once and for all ultimately
decreating the Mind and the Imagination. We shall likely never know
the truth of the matter—the historistic matter—even as we recall that in
"To the One of Fictive Music" (1923) he had early on decreated the
memory of the Virgin, only in that poem to re-create her on his own
terms, thus all the while declining to be a High-Toned Old Christian

Woman.[19] Whatever the details, they will not diminish Stevens's achievement as a poet nor, as important, the intensely humanistic form and content of his poems. Form and content, derivation and commitment, the humanism of the one *in extremis*—such have been my concern in this interpretation.

Let the penultimate words be those of John Berryman, who was perhaps capable, because of his "possibility" as poet, of more scope and compass and human complication than was Stevens but could never get them fully and comprehensively into his poetry. That is, he was a strong poet, yet, as he acknowledges here, subsumed by Stevens as a stronger poet. It is a matter of perfection, realizing one's gift to the fullest. This is the 219th *Dream Song*. "*So Long?* Stevens":

> He lifted up, among the actuaries,
> a grandee crow. Ah he & he crowed good,
> That funny money-man.
> Mutter we all must as well as we can.
> He mutter spiffy. He make wonder Henry's
> wits, though with a odd
>
> . . . something . . . something . . . not there
> in his flourishing art.
> O veteran of death, you will not mind
> a counter-mutter.
> What was it missing, then, at the man's heart
> so that he does not wound? It is our kind
> to wound as well as utter
>
> a fact of happy world. That metaphysics
> he hefted up until we could not breathe
> the physics. *On our side,*
> monotonous (or ever-fresh)—it sticks
> in Henry's throat to judge—brilliant, he seethe;
> better than us; less wide.

A final, doubly exegetical note—doubly exegetical because it would clarify both Berryman's and Stevens's texts: "better than us; less wide." Yes. Because "it is our kind / to wound. . . ." No. Because Stevens does, in fact, wound us. But only, solely, by wounding himself, sacrific-

19. On the possible conversion, in all its evidentiary weirdness, see Peter Brazeau, *Parts of a World: Wallace Stevens Remembered: An Oral Biography* (New York: Random House, 1983), pp. 294-97 and p. 310, n. 6.

ing himself—in his poems, that is—to the tradition of the humanism of
the one.

1977/1979/1986

9

TOWARD THE NEW POETRY:
THE BURDEN OF ROMANTICISM

1

The burden of Romanticism is one that we all bear, however
uneasily. If we can say anything about the modern ego, we can say that
it is romantic—to recall the tautological title of a book by Jacques Bar-
zun published some years ago. We would not have thought of troubling
ourselves so much about the modern ego if Romanticism hadn't discovered it for us, taught us that the sense of ourselves we have when we
face the fact that we are willy-nilly modern is precisely the burden it has
placed upon us. Our egocentricism, even if we think of it as a too
terribly refined version of Renaissance humanism, is at the heart of our
power to have made the kind of world we have made—indeed, to have
made ourselves in that world. Some day, we might have the kind of
philosophical anthropology that will have absorbed the revelations of
our philosophy, psychoanalysis, anthropology, sociology, theory of history, and the like—absorbed those revelations sufficiently to tell us what
we are, where we have come from and how far we have got, where we
turned off the strait road (if we did), and how we might once more get
back on it (if we wish to, if we can, if there is still time). . . . I propose
here a much more modest exercise: to look at the developing situation
of poetry since the later eighteenth century; to focus particularly on the
achievement of "modern" American poetry—that is, the work of those
masters who came into their own between the two world wars; and
then to inquire into the situation of the "new" poetry, "post-modern"
poetry. In order to make such a survey manageable I shall make the
substantial center of my concern poetics: which I take to be the theory
of how poems should—not always do—work, and also of the ground of

authority for their working. In all, I shall be concerned to assess the burden Romanticism has in changing but genetically related ways put upon the poetry on which it has put its stamp. This will be then, within a quite limited purview, an essay in history—or triangulation.

It has been satisfactorily demonstrated, I think, that twentieth-century poetics has been a version, a stage in the development of, romanticist poetics—this despite its so often tendentiously manifest anti-romanticism. For the sake of my argument, I must speak over-schematically, so to sharpen distinctions that are in actuality blurred but are nonetheless there. We can, then, ascribe to that development three stages:

1. The change, beginning more or less toward the end of the eighteenth century, from a "mimetic to a creative conception of poetry"— the mimetic conception being "no longer tenable when men ceased to share the cosmic designs that made mimesis meaningful." What was called for was the sort of poem that "would both formulate its own cosmic syntax and shape the autonomous poetic reality that the cosmic syntax permitted." (I quote and paraphrase some lines from Earl Wasserman's *The Subtler Language*.) Thus the poem as (in Mr. Wasserman's phrase) a "personal world-picture," a myth. Or (in Josephine Miles's phrase) as "the spirit's narrative . . . half-articulated and half-heard, but powerful in its force of implication."

2. The development of a "symbolist" poetics—with its assumption of the isolated poet who gained from his isolation an insight into the need to fuse his world-picture into an image in which the word was one with the thing, and so not amenable to analysis into discursive terms— the poet's isolation putting him safely out of the reach of those who would demand of language that it be commonsensical or "scientific." The symbolist's faith was that his "personal world-picture" was ultimately grounded in a system of extra-human correspondences, insight into which his genius gave him.

3. The development of a modern, "post-symbolist" poetics, in which the symbolizing power of poetry is taken not only as carrying language beyond the purview of ordinary discourse, but also as testing its authenticity as a means of getting beyond, or pointing to something beyond, that purview. When the guarantor of the correspondence of

symbolic structures was taken to be the poet, then perforce the heart of poetry—the essence of poetry—was discovered to be language, words as he could make them into his medium and his only. The outcome of the development was this: the highest test of language was taken to be its possible use in drawing a "personal world-picture," thus of comporting with the poet's archetypal sense of himself as being, before anything else, a person. *Au fond*, one's sense of oneself as a person, the argument went, derived from the certitude that one had no direct access to the things, or persons, of the world; one had only words. Since one wanted more, one had to want more, the question was: How might language be made to transcend language? Or: How might man break out of the confines of language and see what he must see?

To sum up my summing-up: The three stages may be described as having as their central concerns: (1) myth; (2) symbol; (3) language. In actuality, of course, the three concerns—with myth, symbol, and language—have been from the beginning all integrally part of romanticist poetics. Moreover, they are steadily marked, as A. O. Lovejoy some time ago pointed out in his *The Reason, the Understanding, and Time*,[1] by a wholesale delivery of the tasks (especially the epistemological tasks) of philosophy over to poetry—a process that began in immediately post-Kantian (that is, "romantic") philosophy and culminated in the work of Bergson. So that T. E. Hulme's celebrated inauguration, in the name of Bergson, of an anti-romanticist poetics was a surrender camouflaged as a victory. Thus the whirligigs of logic. My point is that in poetics, and accordingly in the practice of poetry, the focus of concern shifts, and at any one stage all three concerns tend to be subsumed under one, that at each of the later stages it is felt—and accordingly acted upon in the making of poems—that the preceding foci of concern have been accommodated to the present ones. We are now, I suspect, overpoweringly aware of the three concerns as comprising at once an evolutionary sequence and an increasingly integrated, perhaps self-identical, group, because we have come to the end of the line whose progress they mark and, confronted by the new poetry, wonder where we go, or will be taken, next.

We so much honor Freud as a central figure in "modernism," it occurs to me, because he tried to find a way of proving that actually the

---

1. (Baltimore: Johns Hopkins University Press, 1981).

concern with myth was only a confused concern with symbol, the concern with symbol only a confused concern with language, and the concern with language in fact only an acceptance—at long last—of the "reality" of the core of our lives day-to-day (and night-to-night): consciousness and the price it demands of us and the rewards it offers. Human dignity, Freud discovered, was (or could be) a product of consciousness—such awareness of one's own history as would, at least in part, free man from being made by it, so that he could make it. With such knowledge we might put into language the record of our learning to live first with ourselves and then with one another. The record, in poetry, would be the act; the meaning, the being. It would be one of the tragic triumphs of consciousness, realizing its fullest—withal limited—capacities for expression and creation; and in doing so, literally, linguistically, discovering its own worth.

Freud's achievement surely has something to do with a curious fact—that, for all the modern poet's announced concern for myth and symbol, he found it increasingly difficult to construct his articles of poetic faith out of them. As is shown by any close and chronologically systematic reading of his poems and his characteristic meditations on poetry, he tried myth and symbol, found them not quite enough, and came to treat them as *means*, not *ends* (or ends-in-beginnings and beginnings-in-ends). This surely is a case where ontogeny recapitulates phylogeny. Herein, functioning as critic, he set the direction for all nonpoets who would be critics too. This, I take it, was, and is, an aspect of his status as culture hero, of his (when he was at his best) heroic honesty. So that he drove himself to seek the grounds of myth and symbol—first by searching for their nature in the workings of the psyche, second by searching for their expressive forms. With the first, he studied "sensibility"; with the second, he studied "language." Inevitably, the first was absorbed into the second, of which it is that special aspect that is of particular interest to poets and their exegetes.

Now, the movement in history from the first stage to the second and from the second to the third has been abundantly studied. I wish here to attend to some aspects of the third, the twentieth-century, the modern, stage—then to inquire into its affiliations not only with what preceded but also with what has followed it.

To do so, I must begin with some cautionary remarks. I must point out that, although we have established as fact the continuity of romanticist poetics into our own time, we cannot thereby read our twentieth-century "romantics" exactly as we read our nineteenth-century "romantics." I say this, because there has been some abortive effort at this self-defeating enterprise—curiously enough, by scholar-critics of Romanticism who somehow forget the prime definition of their field of interest: that it entails, as Professor Lovejoy long ago pointed out, an essential *diversitarianism*; which means that what is interesting and valuable in a poem, even if the poem be presumably grounded in some "universal," is interesting and valuable precisely as the poem is different from other poems—a concretely *differentiated* universal, so to speak.[2]

The diversitarian hope, put at its most general, is expressed in these words of the sociologist Georg Simmel, in a discussion of the achievement of nineteenth-century thought:

> I should like to think that the efforts of mankind will produce ever more numerous and varied forms whereby the human personality may affirm itself and may demonstrate the value of its existence. In fortunate periods, these varied forms may order themselves into harmonious wholes. In doing so, their contradictions and conflicts will cease to be mere obstacles to mankind's efforts; they will also stimulate new demonstrations of the strength of these efforts and lead them to new creations.

Simmel's words (they come from his *Fundamental Problems of Sociology*, 1917)[3] may now seem to us utopian; perhaps they seemed so to him. Romanticism did not in modernism come into its fortunate period. Which is to say that Western culture did not come into its fortunate period. The achievement of our great modernists was to affirm themselves and to demonstrate the value of their own existence—not to affirm their readers and to demonstrate the value of *their* existence: except potentially, as it were. This is an aspect of that overriding alienation which we take to have been (and to continue to be) the great malaise of modern man. Indeed, it was the modern poet's burden to express the symptoms, to teach his readers to discover them in themselves. His diversitarian hope was that as his readers discovered the

2. See "On the Discriminations of Romanticisms," first published in 1924, as reprinted in *Essays in the History of Ideas* (Baltimore: Johns Hopkins University Press, 1948), pp. 228-53.

3. As translated by Kurt Wolff in his *Sociology of Georg Simmel* (Glenco, Ill.: The Free Press, 1950), p. 84.

symptoms, they would learn to survive them, and to be the better for it. For in his malaise, he knew, lay the ground of its own cure. Understanding it, his readers would know what it might mean not to be alienated—their relations to one another, as Emerson had said in "Experience," being casual and oblique. For the poet, the malaise was one of the sensibility; it was characterized by a failure in the sense of community—which made for a failure in the power to communicate. His language had not failed man. Rather, he had failed his language. He had failed to comprehend the power it gave him and also the responsibility possession of such power put upon him. He had failed to see in his use of language a prime means to the ever more numerous and varied forms wherein the human personality might affirm itself and demonstrate the value of its existence.

But perhaps he had not failed entirely. Perhaps he had only been timid, unwilling. Yet perhaps he had forestalled failure by recognizing its threat, its challenge. And in this forestalling the modern poets (romantic, romanticist, neo-romantic) were his leaders. The lesson that their practice—often enough as opposed to their preachment—taught is this:

> Human creativeness in art prevents the recognized varieties of feeling, and established conceptions of the mind, from ever hardening into a final pattern. There are always surprises, the identification of new attitudes and states of mind through freely invented works of art that seem an exact expression of them for the first time. Any closed morality, so far left to itself, is always threatened with this unpredicted shock and disturbance, which suddenly illumines another possibility of human feeling and desire through the invention of a new form of expression. . . . The idea of original art is the idea of an achievement that goes beyond any previous intention, and that must always be to some degree unexpected even by its maker. Even the most confident moralist must know that, sheltered within his own framework of thought, there are many potentially interesting features of behaviour and of feeling which he has not the means to notice. At some time they may be brought to the surface and, through the invention of forms of expression, recognised for the first time. If he reflects, he will acknowledge that these possible revelations must be infinitely many.

These are the words, not of a "neo-Kantian" like Simmel, but of a "Humean"—the "Oxford philosopher," Stuart Hampshire in his

Thought and Action (1959).[4] I quote them not only because they serve to move my argument from a consideration of the diversitarian in general to the diversitarian in particular—in art—but also because they may serve to indicate how the diversitarian faith still universally possesses us. For it characterizes the world that men have together struggled to make during the last two centuries. We quarrel—a Simmel would quarrel with a Hampshire, a Stevens quarreled with an Eliot, a Williams quarreled with them both—not *about* the diversitarian faith but in terms of it.

Thus it was in the nature of the modern poet's vocation, as that "anti-romantic" Ezra Pound had it, that he must again and again "make it new." The notion that twentieth-century Romanticism is sufficiently comprehended by referring it back to nineteenth-century Romanticism—this notion derives from what I should call a "spurious" conception of romanticism, in order to set it against a more tenable conception, centering on the idea of the "diversitarian," which I should call "genuine." (Once more I borrow the terms from Edward Sapir's great essay "Culture: Genuine and Spurious.")[5] Wallace Stevens, a "Romantic" in terms of both consciously held-to doctrine and practice in poetry, put the matter thus in one of his posthumously published *Adagia*:

> It should be said of poetry that it is essentially romantic as if one were recognizing the truth about poetry for the first time. Although the romantic is referred to, most often, in a pejorative sense, this sense attaches, or should attach, not to the romantic in general but to some phase of the romantic that has become stale. Just as there is always a romantic that is potent, so there is always a romantic that is impotent.[6]

Genuine Romanticism and spurious; fresh Romanticism and stale; potent Romanticism and impotent. To discriminate between the one and the other: this perhaps is the historian's real problem. One of the ironies of the history of modernist poetry surely is that poets like Pound and Eliot, the Southern Fugitives, and many of their epigones in the 1940s and 50s—all preached against an impotent Romanticism, a stale Romanticism, a spurious Romanticism, on behalf of one potent, fresh,

---

4. (London: Chatto and Windus, 1959), pp. 246-47.

5. Originally published in 1924, reprinted in *Selected Writings*, ed. David G. Mandelbaum (Berkeley: University of California Press, 1949), pp. 308-31.

6. *Opus Posthumous*, ed. S. F. Morse (New York: Knopf, 1957), p. 180.

and genuine; and claimed thereby to be anti-romantics, even "classicists." The irony, however, is only superficial, and is contained by the fact that the history of literary Romanticism, and other kinds too, is the history of the discovery of the potency of the diverse—if I may make so bold as to combine the language of a Stevens and a Lovejoy. Or: to think of that history in terms of the making of poems—it is the history of a seeking of a means, an authoritative medium, whereby to evoke the potency of the diverse. Modernism—the third stage in the development of Romanticist poetics—centered not on myth or symbol but on language. I think if we get clear the burden of understanding put upon us by the modernist obsession with language, we shall be in a position to comprehend—at least tentatively—the burden of understanding put upon us by the new poetry, and to begin to elucidate its particular obsession, thus its poetics.

I quote from three well-known statements about poetry by modern poets. From T. S. Eliot's "The Social Function of Poetry":

> We may say that the duty of a poet, as poet, is only indirectly to his people: his direct duty is to his *language*, first to preserve, and second to extend and improve. In expressing what other people feel he is also changing the feeling by making it more conscious; he is making people more aware of what they feel already, and therefore teaching them something about themselves.[7]

From Wallace Stevens's "The Noble Rider and the Sound of Words":

> The deepening need for words to express our thoughts and feeling which, we are sure, are all the truth that we shall ever experience, having no illusions, makes us listen to words when we hear them, loving them and feeding them, makes us search the sound of them, for a finality, a perfection, an unalterable vibration, which it is only with the power of the acutest poet to give them. Those of us who may have been thinking of the path of poetry, those who understand that words are thoughts and not only our own thoughts but the thoughts of men and women ignorant of what it is that they are thinking, must be conscious of this: that, above everything else, poetry is words.[8]

From William Carlos Williams's introduction to *The Wedge*:

7. *On Poetry and Poets* (New York: Octagon Books, 1975), p. 9.
8. *The Necessary Angel* (New York: Knopf, 1951), p. 32.

A poem is a small (or large) machine made out of words. . . . When a man makes a poem, makes it, mind you, he takes words as he finds them interrelated about him and composes them—without distortion which would mark their exact significances—into an intense expression of his perceptions and ardors that they may constitute a revelation in the speech that he uses. . . . There is no poetry of distinction without formal invention, for it is in the intimate form that works of art achieve their exact meaning, in which they most resemble the machine, to give language its highest dignity, its illumination in the environment to which it is native.[9]

Now, it is a mere truism to say that poets have always been concerned with words, with language. But this concern has been—or was, say, before the latter part of the eighteenth century—a concern subsidiary to a larger concern: at one extreme, to celebrate in all its rich humanity, and at the other, to denigrate in all its vacuous inhumanity, the ways of men and their gods. (To denigrate is to celebrate inversely, out of a sense of what could or should have been.) The history of literary Romanticism is the history of the gradual metamorphosis of the major concern into the subsidiary, as increasingly that which was to be celebrated—the ways of men and their gods—became not an assured reality, locatable in time and space, anchored in a question-transcending faith, but first a matter of myth, then a matter of symbol, then a matter of language. Those whom this development made unhappy would have said something like "mere" myth, or symbol, or language. Poets have striven to prove that it is not a question of "mere" myth, or symbol, or language; that in man's increasing discovery of the potentiality of his humanity as humanity, understanding the power of myth, or symbol, or language is a sufficient and necessary condition for whatever celebration in art the nature of man allows.

I would characterize the great achievement of modernist poetry, that of the dominating sensibility through World War II, thus: The poet would still celebrate the ways of men and their gods; the testimony of the poems of those writers I have cited is sufficient proof of this. But first he had to celebrate (or denigrate, I repeat), and so enlarge the potential for, man and the ways of man with language, and likewise language and the ways of language with man. Where once the poet could say "proper words in proper places," now he had to say "What words in what places?" Or: "We have words, but no places to put them

9. *Selected Essays* (New York: New Directions, 1969), pp. 256-57.

in; we must make places to put them in." The poet could not simply assume his essential humanity; now he was bound to prove it; prove it linguistically; prove that men were men precisely as they at once used language and were used by it. The traditional function of poetry had been, through its linguistic transformations, to enhance, deepen, and enlarge man's vision of his world and himself in it. Now that function was to make such a vision possible. The vision was not to be attained until after, through his creation of a poetic experience, the poet could not only make us grant the possibility of the vision but also invent for us the ways of realizing it. Words communicate, the implicit argument went, because they are not only the poet's but also the reader's; yet only the poet can tell us what they really mean, how their meaning may be released so that we will all know what they really mean. The great make-believe of most modern poetry was that the reader was composing the poem along with the poet. But then: It turned out not to be *entirely* make-believe. For the reader turned out to have been learning that it was possible, in spite of all the forces that tended to disintegrate and to reduce the languages that might hold modern communities together, to find not only words but also the proper places for them, to use language as a means of realizing oneself as a man—a man perhaps capable even of having gods. (Let me propose schematically that in the history of romanticist poetics through modernism we get this evolving set of oppositions against the forces that disintegrate and reduce man's capacity to make poems: against mechanistic rationalism, the poetics of myth; against positivistic scientism, the poetics of the symbol; against behaviorism and mass communications, the poetics of language.)

Thus it would seem that the characteristic modern poem had as its intention not only registering its substantial concerns but attaining the state, through its working, of an *ars poetica*. (I would here cite as evidence not only the substance but also the mode of *Four Quartets*, the *Cantos*, *Paterson*, *The Bridge*, and "Notes toward a Supreme Fiction," to name only the principal masterworks in this vein.) The poetics of Romanticism had in the twentieth century come to be a poetics wherein, to quote some words of I. A. Richards (from his *Speculative Instruments*), poetry might well be defined as "words so used that their meanings are free to dispose themselves; to make up together whatever they can."[10] Needless to say, perhaps, only a poet could thus free

10. "Poetry as an Instrument of Research," *Speculative Instruments* (Chicago: Uni-

words; and freeing them, put to a specifically linguistic test whatever doctrines they might project, perhaps transform those doctrines in the testing and projecting.

Here we come up against the crucial problem in the modernist version of the romantic theory of poetry. What does it mean to impute agency to words—to say that, freed, as they can be only in poems, they can act freely? Surely this theory of poetry entails a richer and more inclusive linguistics than any we have now; and surely Richards's statement (which he inevitably made the substance of poems) is one that relates the practice of modernist poetry to the contemporaneous practice of philosophy, theology, anthropology, psychology, and the rest—all concerned to understand the meaning of meaning, to preserve against all onslaughts the capacity of language to be meaningful, to understand "textuality." Here the concerns of modernist poetry lay the groundwork for the concerns of "post-modern" poetry. How—to recall Eliot's words—does a poet "extend and improve" language? Why—to recall Stevens's words—is it that the poet can best satisfy our "deepening need for words?" How—to recall Williams's words—can a poet "compose" words "as he finds them interrelated about him" and yet not "distort" them? What is the conception of the meaning of meaning entailed here? What, in short, is the relation between the use of language in poetry and the situation of modern and post-modern man—wherein consciousness of self has become self-consciousness? On what grounds in linguistic theory, not to say ontology and metaphysics, may we place our faith in poetry? Such are some of the issues still raised by modern poetics and the poetry out of which it issues.

Poets, on this argument, had become the unacknowledged *grammarians* of mankind, all the while hoping to be more; but knowing all the while that if they were not this, they were nothing. Romanticism, then, as it issued into twentieth-century poetry, had not necessarily relieved man of the burden of orthodoxy, original sin, history—as has so often been claimed. Nor had it necessarily supplied man with a religion of art to take their place. For these are matters of doctrine; and I am persuaded that one of the lessons to be learned from the history of

---

versity of Chicago Press, 1955), p. 149. In a poem, "Lighting Fires in the Snow," Richards says:

> The wise poem knows its father
> And treats him not amiss;
> But language is its mother. . . .

Romanticism is that its central tenet—the potency of the diverse—transcends doctrines, is a means, an absolute, of testing and judging doctrines, which are relative. So that matters of doctrine comprise a necessary but not a sufficient condition in the practice of most of our great modern poets and may be assented to or denied accordingly—the assent or the denial having no necessary relationship to our estimate of the achievement and value of the poets. The sufficient condition of the practice of poetry is a concern with the viability in language of matters of doctrine as they do and do not manifest the potency of the diverse. Modern poetics, a romanticist poetics, thus considered, meant not to teach man *what* to believe. Rather, it wanted to teach him *how* to believe, the necessary conditions of belief. It instructed him that he could comprehend, and so properly assume, the burden of any doctrine only if he could conceive of it as uniquely, humanly, his own; only if it did not violate his sense of the potency of the diverse; only if he could find the right words for it; only if it would be amenable to poetic expression, so as to be claimable as his own. We don't have to believe a poem, he could say; we have only to believe *in* it.

No modern poet of worth, not even an ostentive romantic, wanted to have his religion split—to recall some cruelly influential, but mistaken, words from T. E. Hulme's "classic" *summa contra* Romanticism. The modern masters wanted just to be sure that it was really theirs; that they could put it into words that comported with their sense of themselves as persons first and wanderers lonely as a crowd second; that, whatever else it might require of them, it would answer to their sense of the potency of the diverse. For they declared that in the potency of the diverse, for them above all latent in the use of language, lay their hope for the dignity not only of *man*, but of *men*: their romantic humanism. This is what they surely have taught the poets who have come after them, the newest poets. For out of the poetics of language, out of the poetics of myth and symbol, there has risen, there is rising, a new, or renewed, poetics—one of statement and, more important, of dialogue. (Which is to say, too long after the fact, that modern, post-symbolist poetics was, for well and for ill, a poetics of monologue.)

2

Are our recent poets (acting, I must emphasize, on our behalf; acting out our struggles to educate ourselves) learning the lesson of their modern masters? I think so—although at this stage I am not altogether clear, because they are not, as to exactly what the lesson is and what, once learned, it will involve. (One never really knows what the lesson is until one has learned it; and then it is part of the sort of history I am sketching now.) We can, as always when dealing with the contemporaneous, mark out "tendencies." I think that it is reasonably clear that in this "post-modern" era we are being moved into a new stage in the history of romanticist poetics, therefore a new stage in the history of ourselves. In the newer poetry—so it seems to me—the sense of an authentic language, authentically used, is somehow strong enough to let poets conceive of themselves as living out their imagined lives in a world whose "public" aspect, however threatening, is not such as to threaten the very existence of poetry itself. It is as though poetry had come through its post-Renaissance phase sufficiently strengthened in ego power to be now capable of putting myth, symbol, and even language where they properly belong—in human space and history, not outside it; as though poetry were once more capable of being poetry, *mere* poetry; as though it were once more ready to stake out its own claim as being a central means whereby man makes not himself but his knowledge of himself; as though "man" as subject were being rediscovered in "reality" as object and vice-versa—so that the subject-object distinction at the heart of romanticist poetics were being dissolved. Accepting the sheer factuality, the sheer givenness, of the human condition, recent poets seem to me to have on the whole ceased trying to explain the world and started to try to know it; and they strive to master, as against being mastered by, implicit principles of explanation (myths, symbols, even their own kind of linguistics). That is, they try to "use" (because they will not be "used by") myth and symbol, and try also to develop the kind of language that, as language should, points beyond itself, even takes the poet beyond himself: from his sense of *man*—as the power of language, being a power of consciousness, may transform it—into a sense of *men*.

A poet like W. D. Snodgrass may remind us at times of Auden, at times of Stevens, at times of many others of his immediate modernist forebears; but he seems to be trying to develop the means whereby he may make statements not about making statements but about objects or events whose import is worth discovering and so stating, not about

the experience of poetry and its ground but about an experience
through poetry and its "significance":

> These trees stand very tall under the heavens.
> While *they* stand, if I walk, all stars traverse
> This steep celestial gulf their branches chart.
> Though lovers stand at sixes and at sevens
> While civilizations come down with the curse,
> Snodgrass is walking through the universe.
>
> I can't make any world go around *your* house.
> But note this moon. Recall how the night nurse
> Goes ward-rounds, by the mild, reflective art
> Of focusing her flashlight on her blouse.
> Your name's safe conduct into love or verse;
> Snodgrass is walking through the universe.
>
> Your name's absurd, miraculous as sperm
> And as decisive. If you can't coerce
> One thing outside yourself, why you're the poet!
> What irrefrangible atoms whirl, affirm
> Their destiny and form Lucinda's skirts!
> She can't make up your mind. Soon as you know it,
> Your firmament grows touchable and firm.
> If all this world runs battlefield or worse,
> Come, let us wipe our glasses on our shirts:
> Snodgrass is walking through the universe.
> ("These Trees Stand . . .")

This just may border on the trivial; the poet may just be using his
capacity as poet to defend himself and his readers against the situation of
which he treats. Snodgrass and his kind may turn out to have been the
Longfellows of our age, as, at the other extreme a poet like Gregory
Corso and his kind, trying to make new the language of all the "mad"
poets from Smart and Blake to Rimbaud and Artaud, may turn out to
have been the Lindsays:

> On the steps of the bright madhouse
> I hear the bearded bell shaking down the woodlawn
> the final knell of my world
> I climb and enter a firey gathering of knights
> they unaware of my presence lay forth sheepskin plans
> and with mailcoated fingers trace my arrival

back back when on the black steps of Nero lyre Rome back I
    stood
in my arms the wailing philosopher
the final call of mad history
Now my presence is known
my arrival marked by illuminated stains
The great windows of Paradise open
Down to radiant dust falls the curtains of Past Time
In fly flocks of multicolored birds
Light winged light O the wonder of light
Time takes me by the hand
born March 26 1930 I am led 100 mph o'er the vast market of
    choice
what to choose? what to choose?
Oh—and I leave my orange room of myth
no chance to lock away my toys of Zeus
I choose the room of Bleecker Street
A baby mother stuffs my mouth with a pale Milanese breast
I suck I struggle I cry O Olympian mother
unfamiliar this breast to me
Snows
Decade of icy asphalt doomed horses
Weak dreams Dark corridors of P.S. 42 Roofs Ratthroated
    pigeons
Led 100 mph over these all to real Mafia streets
profanely I shed my Hermean wings
O time be merciful
throw me beneath your humanity of cars
feed me to giant grey skyscrapers
exhaust my heart to your bridges
I discard my lyre of Orphic futility

And for such betrayal I climb these bright mad steps
and enter this room of paradisical light
emphemeral
Time
a long long dog having chased its orbited tail
comes to grab my hand
and leads me into conditional life
        ("In the Fleeting Hand of Time")

The poems I have quoted run the risks of their makers' romantic
humanism. So does this one by James Wright—which, since it must be
political, refuses to be obliquely or ironically so:

In the Shreve High football stadium,
I think of polacks nursing long beers in Tiltonsville,
And gray faces of Negroes in the blast furnace at Benwood,
And the ruptured night watchman of Wheeling Steel,
Dreaming of heroes.

All the proud fathers are ashamed to go home.
Their women cluck like starved pullets,
Dying for love.

Therefore,
Their sons grow suicidally beautiful
At the beginning of October,
And gallop terribly against each other's bodies.
                ("Autumn Begins in Martin's Ferry, Ohio")

And so does this one, by Gary Snyder—which, since it will confront
the natural world, will strive to penetrate and be penetrated by it:

Pressure of sun on the rockslide
Whirled me in dizzy hop-and-step descent,
Pools of pebbles buzzed in a Juniper shadow,
Tiny tongues of a this-year rattlesnake flicked,
I leaped, laughing for little boulder-colour coil—
Pounded by heat raced down the slabs to the creek
Deep tumbling under arching walls and stuck
Whole head and shoulders in the water:
Stretched full on cobble-ears roaring
Eyes open aching from the cold and faced a trout.
                ("Water")

What strikes me about these poems in contrast to those of their modernist forebears is how carefully they trace out the contours of the experience they would tell us of, so carefully as to make it possibly ours.
Even if they would choose to make out Williams (and also Pound as he
resembles Williams) as their particular master, even if they take themselves to be realizing Williams's concern to create a poem of projective
sympathy, they go beyond Williams. Their forebears—Williams
among them—characteristically fractured or shattered their experiences
and then reconstellated them according to principles dictated by a concern to discover if language could admit them into the sensibility. The
poems I have quoted—two by poets deliberately putting themselves on
a leash, two by poets as deliberately running wild—"do" whereas those

of their forebears "are." The deliberateness is all, perhaps when it should be just enough.

The deliberateness is a product of a deeply felt dialogic relationship with the reader. The mode of control, poem-to-poem, varies enormously, but the end is pretty much the same: to share with, not to talk to, the reader.

John Ashbery makes flat factuality generate a surreal world, almost a world of fantasy but not quite. He will make the familiar unfamiliar, so in the process to know it for what it really, humanly, is:

> I write, trying to economize
> These lines, tingling. The very earth's
> A pension. My life story
> I am toying with the idea.
> I'm perfectly capable (signature)
> The kerosene white branches the stadium
>
> There is no reason to be cold
> Underneath, it is calm today.
> For the moment, clement day
> Observes our transactions with kindly eye.
> There is no reason to suppose
> Anything of the kind will occur.
> I oppose with all the forces of my will
> Your declaration. You are right
> To do so. The street catches auburn
> Reflections, the start is here.
> You may have been well.
> You limit me to what I say.
> The sense of words is
> With a backward motion, pinning me
> To the daylight mode of my declaration.
>
> But ah, night may not tell
> The source! I feel well
> Under the dinner table. He is playing a game
> With me, about credits.
> I have to check in the hall
> About something.
> The invitation arrived
> On the appointed day.
> By nightfall he and I were between.
> The street rages with toil.

Can you let yourself, a moment, put down your work?
(from "Measles")

Richard Brautigan will push the delights of complicit simple-minded-
ness all the way:

> I sit here dreaming
> long thoughts of California
> at the end of a November day
> below a cloudy twilight
> near the Pacific
>
> listening to The Mamas and The Papas
> THEY'RE GREAT
>
> singing a song about breaking
> somebody's heart and digging it!
>
> I think I'll get up
> and dance around the room.
>
> Here I go!
> ("Our Beautiful West Coast Thing")

David Ignatow will annotate with maximum precision a brief encounter and in the same breath (the poem moves that way) make explicit its
implications. The poet's business is no longer a matter of what Eliot
called hints and guesses:

> Say pardon to a bum,
> brushing past him.
> He could lean back
> and spit
> and you would have to wipe it off.
> How would you explain
> that you have insulted
> this man's identity,
> of his own choosing;
> and others could only scratch
> their heads and advise you
> to move on
> and be quiet.
> Say pardon
> and follow your own will
> in the open spaces ahead.
> ("Say Pardon")

And Robert Duncan wills himself to be prophetic; the will powers his poem to its openly cosmic end. Still, the poet faces up to the fact of his limitations, which are his reader's:

> Grand Mother of Images, matrix
> genetrix, quickening in rays
>   from the first days of the cosmos,
>
> turning my poet's mind in tides of
> solitude, seductive reveries, fears, resolves, outrage
>   yet
>   having this certain specific agent I am,
>   the shadow of a tree wavering and yet staying
>
>   deep in it,
>
>   the certain number of days renderd uncertain,
>
>   gathering,
>
>   animal and mammal, drawing such milk
>
>   from the mother of stars.
>   (from "In the Place of a Passage 22")

I have instanced here the work of eight of the "new" poets. Although it avoids classification by schools, peer-groups, manifestos, influences, and the like, the selection is not quite at random. These are, simply enough, some of the new poets whose work I find—in differing degrees, to be sure—compelling. "Compelling" may be too strong a word. I mean just that these are some of the new poets whose work I find myself altogether willing to make part of my own proprioception.

"Proprioception"—the word comes out of psychology—is a central concept in the new poetry, at least for what two poets have made it out to mean. Speaking of his work and that of his peers, Snodgrass said in May 1962:

> We are like the Greeks in this: being great explorers of physical space, they were obsessed with the problem of "limit." How far can you go, they asked, practically and morally?
>
>   The problem of limit, too, encompasses certain psychological problems, especially that of proprioception: the recognition of the self as an object positioned in space relative to other objects positioned in space; or, the self as a subject positioned in space relative to other subjects. But this space must be seen as endless; we must see ourselves as finite danc-

ers on a stage, not infinite, but undefined. This absence of definition gives us a chance to move fully into that relativism proposed so long ago by men like Giordano Bruno, but which so few have dared to explore.[11]

In a coincidence happy for the historian, Charles Olson, a poet who is centrally concerned with "the problem of 'limit,'" was writing, also in May 1962, a vatic manifesto (published in 1965) called *Proprioception*:

> The advantage is to "place" the thing, instead of it wallowing around sort of outside, in the universe, like, when the experience of it is interoceptive: it is inside us/ & at the same time does not feel literally identical with our own physical or mortal self (the part that can die). In this sense likewise the heart, etc, the small intestine etc, are or can be felt as—and literally they can be—transferred. Or substituted for. Etc. The organs.—Probably also why the old psychology was chiefly visceral: neither dream, nor the unconscious, was then known as such. Or allowably inside, like.[12]

". . .limits/are what any of us/ are inside of." Olson writes in the fifth of his *Maximus Poems*. But inside those limits of human space and time, there are available the means of achieving definition through relationship and dialogue, subject to subject. I do not mean here to avoid the issue of the degree to which in their work two poets like Snodgrass and Olson differ. I mean only to indicate how—in their concern to define relationship and dialogue as those of subject to subject, not subject to object—they conceive alike of the vocation of the new poet.

And (since in matters of this importance, one must be quite blunt) I would not deny the dangers of the new poets' way. For striving toward the subject-to-subject relationship, validating the proprioceptive mode, can be an act so strained and desperate as to lead first to the homogenization and then to the annihilation of the sensibility. Expanding the definition of "man," exploring the definition to the utmost—this can lead to an act of suicide mistakenly made out to be a rite of passage. Love of the other may become a totally sentimental, bathetic, confused indulgence of self, and there might be generated a sense of the world in which polymorphism reigns over all. Thus Michael McClure:

11. *Approaches to the Study of Twentieth-Century Literature* (East Lansing: Michigan State University, 1962), pp. 92-93.
12. *Proprioception* (San Francisco: Four Seasons Foundation, 1965), p. 1.

OH BRIGHT OH BLACK SINGBEAST LOVEBEAST CATKIN SLEEK
spined and gullet shaped. Free me
in the tree-lighted evening and full cool
morning. OH
VISION free me erect and huge to VISION
DEEP-DELVED
OUTDELVING. BANNER-
hung and warm warmly gestured
star gestured in
the coldness.
Fingers spread pointing.
The only vision sight-sense.

The appropriate gloss can only be these opening lines from
McClure's "Reflections after a Poem" (the poem being his translation
of Nerval's "Black Spot"):

> LET US THROW OUT THE WORD *MAN*! Such poems as this
> translation of Nerval remind me that I am a MAMMAL! We have
> almost worn out the word *man*. This is the young creature looking into
> the world. The poem makes me see the surge of life. The word MAN is
> not romantic enough!

Thus one extreme example—one phase of the new poetry as it projects itself out of the proprioceptive orbit into absurdity. (The old
humanist rule still holds: Everything ventured, nothing gained.) But
even as we are aware of this danger, this risk, unwisely and unin-
telligently (that is the key word!) courted, we must remember that it
will in the long run be the orbit that matters. It is that orbit which I
have been trying to trace in this essay—that orbit, and as I have said, the
sense of the new poet's vocation which it defines, the poetics which it
articulates. Within this poetics are the facts of our case as the new
poetry lets us confront them.

Moreover, if we were to look at the later work of poets a generation
or so older, poets "transitional" between the "modern" and the
"new"—Berryman, Shapiro, Lowell, Warren, Schwartz, Roethke, for
example—we would find analogous "proprioceptive" qualities and
conditions: a turning to narrative forms, explicit or implicit; an attending to states of consciousness as they are implicated in action; an increasing sense of inter- (as opposed to intra-) personal relations; an exploding

diversity, a sometimes awkward honesty, a directness, an openness; a search for the face behind the persona. We would perhaps be surer of this poetry than of that I have quoted. But the aim of this essay is to suggest how, even as we reconsider briefly that of which we may be fairly sure, we may try out unsureness. Secure in the history our poets have made, we may well risk being insecure in the history they are making. Nonetheless, the qualities and conditions I have noted are there, in older poets and younger. And the reader is no longer a hypocrite, peeping over the poet's shoulder, hoping against hope not to have to acknowledge that he is the poet's double, his brother—but rather that he can be one whom the poet would encounter, with whom he would initiate a dialogue. Language becomes a medium *for* as well as a medium *in*. Myth and symbol are parts of the poet's vocabulary, not its formal, much less final, cause.

It is, then, as part of their essential heritage from Romanticism that poets of the generation of Eliot, Stevens, and Williams, our great "Moderns," took upon themselves the obligation to preserve, refine, and extend our language. Their destiny was to teach poets of following generations to use it in such a way that they, or their progeny, might one day be audible witnesses to that great romantic vision: the transformation of the humanism of the one into the humanism of the many. Just at the point in history when the material conditions of life may, at their level, make this transformation possible, such conditions bring to bear a power for dehumanization that might, as well, make it impossible on other, higher levels. It will be possible, of course, only if a power for humanization is brought to bear. And the poet is ready, as in the nature of his relation to his society he is always ready. He has his language, which incorporates his understanding of symbol and myth and the ideas of order projected thereby. But he wants to discover and project his own idea of order, to walk through his own and his fellows' universe and to know the conditional life. For him symbol and myth can be no more than heuristic, although it is quite true that the evidence of his work shows often that his poems know this better than he does. He senses that at some point he must shed his Hermean wings and discard his lyre of Orphic futility. He will make his firmament grow touchable and firm. He will declare quite flatly "therefore." He will make his dizzy hop-and-step descent. He will take the whole earth to be his pension. He will get up and dance around the room. He will say Pardon, so that

he may follow his own will. He will seek his and his fellows' Grand
Mother of Images. Language, he has been given to discover, is to talk
with. And if talking about oneself is inevitable, still it is important not
to talk only to oneself. Too, it is important to listen.

For the poet knows what his magus knows: "that an individual life is
the accidental coincidence of but one life cycle with but one segment of
history; and that for him all human integrity stands and falls with one
style of integrity of which he partakes."[13] The magus I quote is Erik
Erikson—one psychoanalyst who, in practice and theory, shows that he
understands the sort of goal which, for all their strained deliberateness
(a kind of reaction-formation?) the poems I have quoted point toward.
This shouldn't surprise us, however. For psychoanalysis is the modern
ego's best account of itself. Just as recent poetry has striven to initiate its
true dialogue with the world, so has recent psychoanalysis.

I have a sense that the poet would now use his language so as to
humanize—perhaps to make symbol and myth human, perhaps to discover that they are after all human and are therefore our means, in
poetry and out, of discovering and so accepting and enlarging our
humanity. The poet is still the kind of utopian we need, the utopian of
the present. He is the last romantic, as has been virtually every poet
since the later eighteenth century at least. For he knows that it is in the
nature of very phase of Romanticism that it be the "last," if its artists
are continually to actualize the potency of the diverse. In art, the last
shall always go first.

Theodore Roethke, an older and probably a wiser poet than the ones
I have so far quoted, called one of his books *Praise to the End!* The phrase,
of course, is Wordsworth's; the passage is from *The Prelude* (1.346-350).
Taken out of its essentially symbolic, mythic context, so that it renders
just Wordsworth's all too human sense of himself, it marks the tone and
substance, the characteristic import, not only of Roethke's poetry but
also of that of many of his younger contemporaries, whose future was
in his bones:

> . . . How strange, that all
> The terrors, pains, and early miseries,
> Regrets, vexations, lassitudes interfused
> Within my mind, should e'er have borne a part,

13. *Identity: Youth and Crisis* (New York: Norton, 1968), p. 140.

And that a needful part, in making up
The calm existence that is mine when I
Am worthy of myself! Praise to the end!

I have said that the passage is here quoted out of context. And I have shifted the context even more by speaking not of Roethke and his generation, but of the generation of Snodgrass, Corso, Wright, Snyder, Ashbery, Brautigan, Ignatow, Duncan, and (alas) McClure. But then, this is what Romanticism has done—steadily shifted modern man's context, until at last he can hope to be capable at once of finding a proper context and making it his own, of accepting no context unless he can in poems and all his creative endeavors know it as his own. It is of the essence of the latest phase of Romanticism that he should have discovered that his context is not his own unless it is his fellows', and not theirs unless it is his. Perhaps it will turn out to be God's—but surely not unless it is at least man's. At least. And the terrors, pains, miseries, regrets, vexations, lassitudes are not only within man's mind but also without. The boon of a calm existence must be not only his but also his community's. We have been true enough to the burden Romanticism has put upon us to have invented—that is, at once discovered and created—a poetics of dialogue. The poet speaks, so to be spoken to, so to speak again . . . Praise to the end!

1971

INDEX